Healthy recipes

Michel Biehn's

Healthy recipes

International cuisine from a provençal table

Photography by
Gilles Martin-Raget

Flammarion

To Christine and Michel Guérard,
the true masters of healthy eating
and the art of living

Contents

I had just turned fifty and I weighed 280 pounds and I had had enough. However, it was not as if I was just sitting around. I was working hard, huffing and puffing, my back straining. It seemed that I wore the extra weight well, as my friends always reassured me: "It suits you, being so big. It's part of your character." To bypass the problem of the devastating gaze of vendors as they systematically announced, smiling, that they did not "have my size," I would dress in large ponchos, Indian pajamas and Uzbek *chapans* brought back from my travels. I would hold forth about the true nature of beauty and elegance, how loose-fitting clothing afforded more freedom, and how narrow cuts were constricting. To justify my indulgence with food, I would write cookery books.

I had not always been so large, however. Up till the age of thirty, I was very thin, gangly as a stork, with the delicate musculature of a Dogon warrior. I floated on air, without a care in the world, free from responsibility and constraint. In those days it was the time to make choices, take gambles, start fighting, taste first victories, the first house, children, one after the other. With each pregnancy, I put on weight in tune with Catherine. We laughed about it then, joking about a phantom pregnancy. But I never actually lost weight again, not in any lasting way, despite several attempts to diet. On the contrary, I settled comfortably into my upholstered mass. For a time I felt sheltered there, but one day I realized that this sense of comfort was merely illusory. Everything proved stronger than me—the difficulty of maneuvering in a world rolling onward, the stress this brings with it, the heavy childhood baggage that must be dragged painfully around until we feel brave enough to open it and face the wounds and scars, ghosts and demons, of all shapes and sizes. The awareness that such suffering is actually the common lot of all humanity does nothing to soothe or console. So, with the help of a therapist, I undertook a long analysis of myself, at the end of which, among other discoveries, I understood the deep-seated reasons that had led me to build up this mattress of fat I had become. From then on, I felt that I could do without it. But I was fifty years old and weighed 280 pounds. I had at least 65 pounds to lose. How I managed is the subject of this book.

I took a long exploratory journey through the land of dieting, from Macrobiotics to Instinct Therapy, from Montignac to Atkins, via Zero percent and Low-Calorie labels, the Crete Diet, Germinated Cereals, Saint John's Wort, and pineapples. I read more than fifty books written by

This whole tale takes place in a marvelous Provençal house, where patios and gardens abound, offering perfect corners for feasting al fresco. In the lower orchard, the cherry trees are dressed in flamboyant fall colors, providing the perfect setting for a delightful picnic.

the high priests of diet food—doctors for the most part, who scientifically prescribe, argue, and recommend anything and everything while contradicting all things in between, until you feel they are actually writing in Latin. For twenty years, I had tried different methods on myself. The least oddball of them was to observe carefully not only variations in weight, but also the ways in which my body and mood reacted to the often draconian treatments I inflicted on myself. The large majority of such diet theories are, at heart, unbalanced. There are "permitted" foods and "permitted" ways of preparing them, but the ensuing blandness feels like self-punishment, while the lack of variation leads to gloom and unbearable tedium, as well as inevitable nutritional shortfalls. And then there are the "outlawed" foods, like chocolate and butter, sugar or bacon, and "forbidden" methods of food preparation, such as deep-frying, the abolition of which only increases frustration. The most spot-on and effective theory is possibly that of calorie counting. But it's like the old question, "What weighs more: a ton of feathers or a ton of lead?" Fifty calories of chocolate are, after all, no more detrimental to the figure than fifty calories of steamed zucchini. The apparently insurmountable difficulty to me was embarking on these calculations on a daily basis while still trying to cook balanced and varied meals. I was and still am incapable of going into the kitchen armed with scales, calculator, paper, and pen.

Some of these adventures were actually awesome ordeals. Ultimately, and despite several spectacular and rapid bouts of weight loss, they always ended in failure. However, they provided valuable experience in dietary matters and enabled me, when the moment came, to elaborate a new way of eating. I was thus able to lose seventy-seven pounds and find a new stable weight with very little difficulty, without frustration, excesses, or shortfalls, and without experiencing dieting as a punishment. This means that today I feel good about myself and perfectly healthy. To maintain this wellbeing, I have drawn on cookery from all around the world to find recipes compatible with this balance. I have modified some when I could do so without distorting them, and I have invented others. My friends have done the rest, offering me their own recipes. Never have I cooked so much, turning the process of weight loss into a feast. Slimming has truly become synonymous with pleasure for me.

I am not going to mention "dieting" again. The book is not about periodic changes to eating patterns that whittle off pounds in no time. This is fairly easy with a little determination, but they only slip back on again as soon as we resume "eating normally," as we surely have to do. The real point is to change how we eat for good. I recommend that you should enjoy doing so; indulge yourself while discovering new pleasures. Start by asking yourself what "eating normally" actually means for you at the moment. Over the course of a week, try the following experiment – note down *everything* you eat and drink throughout the day, right down to the smallest square of cheese and the tiniest peanut, and to the smallest glass of lemonade or wine; note down how much, when, and in what way.

It is likely you will be very surprised with what you discover in your notebook at the end of the week. You will maybe notice you eat too much cheese, too much buttered toast, too few vegetables, and never any fish. Maybe you have not bitten into an apple for years. Perhaps you stand in front of the refrigerator and gobble down a starter a half-hour before your main meal. Or you finish off the remains of a meal on the honorable pretext that not a crumb should be wasted, almost to the point of finishing off

In the herb garden, basking beneath the open sky, mint and chives are at hand, while from the nearby hill aromas of thyme and rosemary waft over, mingling with the scent of wysteria.

leftovers from guests' plates: "How," after all, "could anybody leave all that delicious potato gratin?" Maybe, when eating out, you take a mouthful or two from others' plates, out of curiosity, for the taste. Maybe you have a little hole that needs filling just before bedtime and tuck into the remains of the lasagna—it is even better cold. You totally forget to drink between meals and so you make up for it at the dinner table. What is more, you do not even like water. You have trouble digesting peppers and raw onions, yet you serve yourself a huge second helping of *salade niçoise* and wash it down with Coca-Cola. I do not exaggerate. These are all things I have done! But do not panic, and do not feel guilty; it only hurts and it gets you nowhere. You are going to change while learning how to be good to yourself. Make

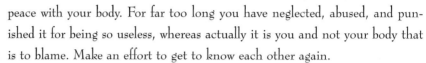

peace with your body. For far too long you have neglected, abused, and punished it for being so useless, whereas actually it is you and not your body that is to blame. Make an effort to get to know each other again.

At about the same time I undertook this great enterprise, I discovered Istanbul. It is a magnificent town that is friendly and cosmopolitan, where nobody is really a stranger. The hospitality of the people in the old part of the city is flawless, and Turkish cuisine is light, natural, and very balanced—but we will come back to this. Everything about Istanbul enchanted me: the light on the Bosphorus, changing and beautiful at all hours of the day, the elegance of the mosques, the aroma of apple-scented tobacco emanating in wisps and coils from the *nargilehs*, the beauty of Isnik faience in the Topkapi harem and in the mosaics of the Church of the Holy Savior of Chora, and the gentleness of the air. One evening, leaving the Grand Bazaar, having viewed a good hundred carpets, nibbling on exquisite, tiny almonds fresh from faraway Samarkand, and supping incredible amounts of tea, I found myself at the door of a *hammam*. The sign said: "Historic Turkish bathhouse built by Sinan." Sinan was Sultan Suleiman the Magnificent's famous architect, who built no fewer than forty-two mosques in the town of Istanbul. There was an irresistible cultural argument in favor of seeing this: for the first time ever, I dared enter a *hammam*. I soon found myself nearly naked, with a *pestma*—a rectangle of checked cotton—rolled simply around the waist (this suits slender physiques well, but was, alas, a little too small for my stout figure). I was tempted to tug it downward, then burst out laughing thinking of how women in the sixties would persist in pulling at their mini-skirts in an attempt to hide their knees. I shook off my apprehensions and set out on the adventure.

I left the lounge and crossed the masseurs' zone, demarcated by a high rampart of piled towels. They were sitting in line on a bench, eyeing up clients as girls in a bordello might, weighing up their bodies

When the sun beats down at the height of day, summer lunches are eaten
in the cool shade of the arbor. Here is a prime vantage point to contemplate the flower garden,
where exuberantly growing fig and olive trees bring a sense of freedom to the tame
and orderly rows of trimmed box trees.

as well as their wallets. One of them stood up and asked in a deep voice: "Massage?" And without waiting for a reply, he took from my hand the yellow plastic token that I had been given at the cash desk. Then he shoved me in front of him, quite roughly, into an ugly, icy-cold room. I was already feeling quite disappointed and was wondering why I had come when I pushed open a second heavy wooden door. It was as though I had gone through a looking glass. The space before me seemed both circular and vertical. At the center, there

was an octagonal, gray marble platform. All around were seven small lateral chapels, also with marble-clad floors and walls. They were furnished with three large stone basins containing water. The air was saturated with hot vapor, through which bright parallel shafts of light glanced, beaming in from outside through glass apertures set in a huge dome that, way up above, crowned the scene. The openings allowed sunlight to enter and caress a shoulder or leg as it nonchalantly relaxed on the polished marble beach. There were a dozen or so men. A father and son were rapt in conversation while washing themselves meticulously in a rich soapy lather. A little farther on, an old man tottered with great effort, taking small, even steps, his lips mouthing the words of a long, silent monologue. A large man was stretched out on his back. His huge belly—like a beached jellyfish clinging to driftwood—seemed to be independent from his otherwise small, dry body. In one of the apsidal rooms, two cheerful young men were laughing; the huge sound cascaded round the recesses of the edifice. A tall, ginger man in his forties was busy doing stretching exercises, which appeared even more difficult given the heaviness of the air, while next to him a small, squat man with brown hair, covered evenly from head to toe in a velvety, blue-tinged down, froze in flattering poses that he repeated slowly and regularly.

The steam, while it muffled sounds, also cast a veil over the scene. It was peculiar and paradoxical that the lack of privacy there actually afforded such perfect solitude. I was absorbed by the novelty of the scene, but noticed that I was alone in paying attention to my surroundings, and felt almost embarrassed for my indiscretion. But the awkwardness I felt about showing my too-fat body disappeared. I let myself go to the mood of the moment and lay out voluptuously on the polished marble. It was at this point that the

In their huge ornamental vases, placed in the garden for the sunny season,
orange trees fill the air with the fragrance of their flowers; their golden fruit brighten the foliage
with shining points of light. Fresh water flowing from the fountain mingles musically
with the rustle of leaves, providing the lunch table with the finest of beverages.

massage started. While Hassan's firm hands connected my consciousness to my body, his gentle warm voice rose in a sublime *melopoeia*, an ancient song of Anatolia, which gently silenced all laughter and chatter. It seemed to me that, united by the beauty of the site and carried along by this voice, in unison we came into contact with God.

This experience in the *hammam* triggered my metamorphosis. From that moment on, I decided to eat less, then to eat differently. I dared to go to a gym, and while the first weeks were an awesome ordeal, I quickly discovered the pleasure of moving, running, watching my body change from week to week, and finally making demands on myself that I had never before made.

The week that followed my return from Istanbul I was busy providing catering, interior decor, and furnishings for a divine place situated high up in a Provençal village, as pretty as all those villages are. Around a hanging garden sprawled a set of buildings that successively over the centuries had served as a fortress and garrison headquarters, a convent, then as a seigniorial mansion. This had created, in the guise of a village house, a breathtaking architectural folly. High, crisscross vaults led the way to a small Directoire-style dining room, flanked by boudoirs decorated in Romany style, at the end of which was a monumental staircase complete with balusters and pilasters, climbing straight to a fairytale attic and watchtower. Successive additions and embellishments had stopped at the end of the eighteenth century, leaving this magnificent setting in poor repair, but miraculously preserved from any recent architectural felony.

It took more than two years to restore it; two blissful years spent with its owners, my friends Frankie and Tench. Frankie is a woman of style and taste and of rare elegance in any situation. She is both wildly cheerful and exacting, eccentric and absolutely charming, demanding as much from herself as she does from everybody, never renouncing her quest for perfection. My encounter with this exceptional woman changed my life. The bright complicity we quickly struck up seemed to be a telltale sign, leading me to find the best of myself. This vast undertaking progressed like a game, a radiant, light-hearted exchange that never let me breathe easily, pushing me to my limits, where I was surprised to discover new resources. I would like to take the opportunity to pay homage to this wonderful magician, my mentor and friend. Despite the scale of the refurbishment, Tench and Frankie still lived in the house, switching camp from room to room like officers in battle, welcoming their friends lavishly among the ladders and bags of cement. I will never forget the candlelit dinner where we covered everything potentially unsightly with ecru hemp sheets. Installed at the center of the construction site, two large round tables sagged beneath the weight of silverware, surrounded by dressers with a collection of Chinese porcelain, the blue of which provided the only hint of color in this ivory and plaster-dusted setting. It was enchanting. And the harmony that reigned swept away all dissonance. This is what the art of living is all about.

*On the terrace, parasols, cushions, and overflowing jars of flowers
are set out ready for the feast*

THE PLEASURES OF LOSING WEIGHT

15

Style and imagination, far from being futile subjects, seem to me to be the essential ingredients for happiness. It is with great pleasure that I can share this house with you today, as all the photos in the book were taken there. This adventure and its demands, its difficulties and victories brought about my own transformation as well as that of the setting.

What is this method then? And how may pleasure ever be found in that which seems so much its opposite? Obviously, losing weight relies on eating less, and being healthy relies on eating better. As for pleasure, which is indispensable to the success of the undertaking, it should be found in refinement, in a quest for quality and subtlety rather than greed and excess. We should eat what we like, in smaller quantities. We are therefore well advised to choose low-calorie foods because they allow us to have larger servings. There are many ideas that should be consigned to the past: that indulgence is a sin, and dieting is its punishment; that a diet should be severe, austere, and bland, or even plain bad if it is to work; that all good things are the devil's work; that eating healthy, balanced meals and banishing indulgence for ever is incompatible with fine cuisine and the divine gourmet pleasures that inevitably make one flesh out, obese, and diabetic, sending cholesterol levels sky high. Here I intend to prove quite the contrary: that a happy balance—including indulgence—is possible, and that it is within our grasp. Here, then, are several very simple but firm rules, along with some advice:

Accept the idea that you have to kick your bad habits. This is the key! If this book interests you—whether you have eight or eighty pounds to lose, or if you have digestive troubles—it will be because you have adopted bad habits. You just have to change them. So get ready for the adventure.

If your weight problem is serious, consult a nutritional expert. My sole hope is that this book helps you find, in tandem with the specialist, a new art of living.

Eat three meals a day, to which you might possibly add one snack. Breakfast is indispensable. It is the meal that is least detrimental to the figure, the one that will be best metabolized, so it provides the perfect moment to indulge. Later I will give you a number of suggestions for breakfasts depending on the season and the program of your day. However, breakfast should be a real meal, eaten in peace, so you should wake a little earlier, decorate your breakfast table with a rose, and start the day in style. Lunch should also be a real meal, and not a sandwich eaten hurriedly standing up. However, the evening meal should be light, the lightest of the three. The major difficulty then is "eating out." We will talk about that later, but with a little training you can manage fine.

No nibbling. It is simply a bad habit that often has nothing to do with hunger. Try to make each of your real meals a pleasant occasion where you wallow in such contentment that it will help you discipline yourself and wait for the next meal. If, nevertheless, you are tempted by a demon craving,

The patch of lawn beside the swimming pool
makes an attractive setting for lunch.

or have a "little hole to fill" between meals, drink a large glass of mineral water. If this does not appease it, call on your demon pride within you and tell yourself that you have exceptional strength of character and you can resist temptation, then leave the two fiends to fight it out between themselves. If this does not work, have an apple, or a stick of celery.

You need a little of everything. Try to find a balance. In other words, find all the elements necessary to maintain good health in the meals you eat. Not eating some foods inevitably creates shortfalls that can be harmful to health, never mind that it also creates nagging frustration. There are no "devil" foods, as long as you select fresh, healthy, good quality produce. However, absolutely avoid eating any industrially made culinary preparation of the type that requires an experienced chemist to understand its composition. When you go shopping, learn to read the labels. If you do not understand them, put the packet quickly back on the shelf.

Make the most of simple, fresh produce that is good and ripe, at the height of its season, and not force-grown artificially in greenhouses with excessive use of fertilizers. If you do, you will be so delighted with the excellence of its flavor that you will not think twice about eating it raw to revel in its taste and goodness. After all, vitamins, as we all know, are depleted by cooking. This goes of course for lettuces, carrots, tomatoes, cucumbers, and radishes, for fennel, celery, and scallions, but also for tender zucchini and young artichokes, cabbages, peas, young fava beans, and baby snow peas, all germinated cereal grains—and even fish and meat.

Variety is not only a guarantee of balance; it is also an excellent palliative to frustration. One of the wonders of the world today is that almost all its products have become readily accessible. The age is long gone when we could only eat regional produce, or when children were offered oranges at Christmas as a rare, exotic delicacy. Cardamom and saffron from Kashmir, salmon from Scotland, buffalo-milk mozzarella, bulgur wheat from Anatolia and spelt from Pays de Sault, balsamic vinegar from Modena, Sichuan pepper, and Tuscan or Baux Valley olive oil, pumpkins, and parsnips: all of these can be bought, whether you live in Marseilles, London, or San Francisco. The time has come then to banish monotony, to be creative and curious, to explore textures and flavors and untried tastes, and to find in this infinite range a new motivation for your desire for food.

On the other hand, it is essential to be able to moderate how much you eat. Here are several tricks to help you do this. Try to eat slowly, a little more slowly than you're used to, thinking about what you are doing. It is surprising what is gobbled down in a meal without even noticing, carried away by momentum, so-called indulgence, or by the flow of conversation. As soon as you catch yourself

In the small dining room Chinese porcelain frames a vegetable terrine.
"Here, everything is order and beauty, luxury, calm, and voluptuousness,"
as Baudelaire says.

shoveling the food down, stop for a moment, calm down, breathe deeply, and start again, calmly. Georges Oshawa, the high priest of macrobiotics, used to say that every mouthful should be chewed fifty-one times. Without going this far, the fact of chewing enables better digestion and assimilation of food. Furthermore, it should help you become aware of the moment when you are full, when your legitimate hunger ceases to guide you, and the point at which you could easily let yourself go too far. At this precise moment, stop everything, place your fork on your plate, regardless of however many mouthfuls remain, and do not touch them. Respect for yourself is more valuable than any consideration you might give these remnants. Here is one last rule, particularly relevant when you dine among friends: try everything and do not take second helpings.

But not all at the same time. You do not have to find nutritional balance in one single meal, or in every meal, or even over a single day. You might very well eat, for example, wholegrain bread or cereals for breakfast, crudités, meat or fish and vegetables at midday, with a fruit snack and nice risotto in the evening. However, avoid mixing foods containing animal proteins and carbohydrates in the same meal. Only vegetables, which contain fiber, can combine well with each of these. This is important and is worth dwelling on. Foods can be classed into three categories. The first is animal proteins: meats, fish, shellfish, and seafood (choose fish and seafood over meat, and poultry over red meat), eggs, and all dairy produce. The second encompasses carbohydrates—bread, pasta, rice, all grain cereals, and derivatives such as bulgur wheat, couscous, and oatmeal; dried pulses such as chick peas and lentils; legumes such as fava beans, peas, and green beans; vegetables such as potatoes, sweet potatoes and, to a lesser extent, squashes and artichokes; seeds and nuts such as walnuts and almonds. And finally, in the third category, come all fresh fruit and vegetables, apart from those mentioned in the second category. In one meal, any first category food can be mixed with a third category food. In another, you may mix second and third, but never first and second. This approach was pioneered twenty years ago by, I believe, a Californian dietician, whose name I forget. May he forgive me and accept our eternal gratitude. The joy of this way of eating is that no food is excluded. We can thus eat until full, whether our penchant is for pasta, potatoes, or chickpeas, as long as they are not smothered in melted butter and as long as we postpone the roast guinea fowl to the following meal. It is on this very simple principle, consisting of alternating vegetarian meals with meals featuring meat or fish and vegetables, that the recipes of this book have been based.

There is one more terrifying combination—that of fat and sugar, whether in savory or sweet foods. What do we mean by fats and sugars here? In general, you should avoid all animal fats. If you like

The elegance of the table contributes as much to the overall pleasure
as do the subtle flavors of the dishes.

butter, buy excellent quality butter and eat it uncooked, from time to time, in small quantities. Cream should only make very rare appearances on your table. However, you can use soy cream instead, a non-dairy cream made of soybeans, available in most organic grocery stores. While not really replacing cream, or crème fraîche, as nothing can replace their subtle taste, it does work wonders in dishes, from blanquette of veal to *gratin dauphinois*. It will feature often in our recipes. Duck fat is excellent; use it from time to time to sauté mushrooms, for example. However, save bacon for rare moments of madness and refer to chapter seven: "Several recipes for the morning after." Rid yourself of margarine for good, even low-fat margarine, and any other industrial preparation of the same kind.

Prepare most of your cooking with olive oil, which is as healthy uncooked in salads as it is for browning, sautéing, stewing, grilling, and even frying. You may also use other first cold-pressed vegetable oils. This said, and as good as it is for the health and on the palate, olive oil is composed of 100 percent lipids like all other oils. You should learn to consume it in moderation. For a salad sauce, for example, if two soupspoons are enough to coat your greenery with the gentle flavor of the oil, it is pointless, and detrimental to your figure, to add a third, or even a fourth. Stop pouring oil directly from the bottleneck and equip yourself with one of those marvelous pouring funnels that allow you to drizzle olive oil in a perfectly controlled way.

As far as sweet sugars are concerned, like fats, there are some that are better than others. Best of all are fruits and the form of sugar they contain—fructose. Right behind comes honey, an excellent natural product. Next comes unrefined cane sugar: with its delicious taste, interesting consistency, and beautiful color, it is perfect for sweetening cottage cheese, French *fromage blanc,* or yogurt. The big loser, the sugar to avoid, is refined white sugar. It is, however, indispensable for pastries and jams. Personally, I am not fond of sugar substitutes, and I prefer to go without and enjoy the full flavor of coffee, tea, and hot chocolate. It was a little strange at first, but then came the discovery of the subtle underlying flavors, and now I would never think of adding sugar.

Whether served at the table or at a picnic on the grass,
a good wine is an excellent healthy natural drink. You should try to drink less,
sipping slowly, making the most of the multiple sensations of each mouthful.

So sugars and fats do the figure no favors. The important thing is to reduce their intake drastically and, in any case, to not mix them, or as little as possible. However, here lies the problem—delicious pastries would not be possible without mixing butter and sugar or almond and honey together. So save such indulgences for special meals: these are as indispensable a part of your balanced diet as all the other rules I have laid down.

Have one rest day per week. Once a week, loosen your shackles and let yourself eat what you miss the most: comfort foods such as burger and fries, a nut sundae, or some spur-of-the-moment fancy. Why deny yourself that local beef specialty while on holiday, or why upset your dear aunt by refusing to eat her fantastic lamb casserole? Apparently Buddha said that anything that had been prepared and offered with love should be accepted with love. He would therefore make an

exception and eat meat when it was offered to Him, even though He had made a vow against it to respect life.

This said, if you are very keen to lose weight, do not include a rest-day at the beginning of your adventure. Instead, wait a month or two, until you have settled into your new habits, before including these beneficial rest-days. And when you do, while such periodic straying or excess should not make you feel guilty, you should not, by the same token, suddenly start stuffing yourself with fatty foods and pastries. An excellent method to adopt generally is never to take second helpings. It is essential to regain control the following day and perhaps be a little stricter that day.

Learn how to taste things again. This goes hand in hand with selecting quality seasonal produce. A ripe, flavorsome strawberry in the month of June has no need for sugar or cream. The meat of a free-range chicken, fed on seeds and other tasty morsels foraged from the grass, is so flavorsome that it makes a delicious roast without adding marinades or sauce. Frankly, rather than adding sugar to unripe bland strawberries, I would rather tuck into a pear or a bunch of grapes. You should rediscover the pleasure of going to market, meeting growers, choosing vendors who love their job. Cheese-sellers who refine their own cheese, bakers who knead their own dough, and fish-sellers who will explain to you the difference between wild salmon and farmed salmon: people like this are all around you. Their products are more expensive, I hear you say. It is true. But you do not have to eat cheese or meat at every meal. Why not buy excellent quality products, less often? For other meals, you may feast simply on a rocket salad

and two free-range eggs, or on a simple potato, boiled in its skin, with a pinch of coarse salt and a dash of olive oil. The quality of the fare allows for frugality and simplicity.

Today's food habits involve a reduction in the range of flavors and textures. Bitter or sour flavors are often considered disagreeable, whereas not long ago we would relish a dandelion salad or ripe persimmon fruit. Meanwhile, bland food seems to herald a frightening void and we eagerly add as much salt and sugar as we can. However, such foods allow a break between savory and sweet courses. Tart flavors are considered too brutal; we prefer slightly acidic foods. Spicy food terrifies us even if its exoticism is appealing. Strong, pronounced flavors are eclipsed by neutral ones that we would like to believe are subtle. Food today has to be soft and "tender," so we go for creams, mousses, emulsions, purées, and stews. There are many sensual pleasures to be had in crunchy, hard foods. The spoon is busily replacing the fork. Not only is this a fault of taste, but to my mind it is leading to culinary impoverishment. So, before you automatically reach for the salt or pepper mill, and before you feel exasperated when you have to chew a little when eating octopus, say, I would really encourage you to give those flavors and textures that surprise you the time to win you over.

Discovering the true taste of things does not mean, of course, banishing aromatic herbs, spices, and condiments from your kitchen. On the contrary, in the course of this book, not only are we going to use herbs and spices in abundance, but I will also suggest you use certain "expensive" foods, like truffles, in very small quantities, to flavor eggs or a salad, or "rich" foods, like parmesan or Roquefort cheese, as condiments to spice up vegetables or a plate of pasta. Spices and condiments are not there to replace the flavor of things or mask their blandness, but to bring out elegant and subtle alliances, to accentuate, punctuate, or bring feeling.

Drink a lot between each meal. So far we have only talked about eating. So what about drinking? Be aware that while you should drink a lot of water between meals and throughout the day, because it helps your body eliminate fats and toxins, you should refrain from doing so during meals so as not to swell the stomach.

The best drink is water, of course: mineral or spring water. If you drink mineral water, all producers agree, you should change brand regularly as their compositions vary—their tastes, too. Today water comes in considerable varieties and from faraway countries. Enjoy tasting them and make your own selection of brands to alternate at the dinner table.

Wine is an excellent, natural, healthy drink. The problem is that it contains sugar and that sugars fix fats. You should thus limit your consumption. Select good wines and drink less, sipping slowly,

Harmony can be found everywhere, even in the closet. The crockery here is arranged as in a still life, with an elegance that makes you forget to close the door.

making the most of the multiple sensations of each mouthful. Personally, I save wine for the evening meal, and have just one or two glasses.

Save beer to accompany sauerkraut with meat, or to have with meals in Vietnamese or Japanese restaurants. If you like sugar-free colas, as I do, keep them for really extravagant meals. Apart from these, you should avoid industrial sodas, cordials, and other appetizers. Drink herbal teas, green or black teas, hot or iced, as much as you want, as these are only flavored water.

Vitamin-rich fruit juices are perfect before breakfast.

Find a sport you enjoy. It can be walking, swimming, pumping iron, dancing, boxing, rowing, cycling, running, table tennis, climbing, anything you want, but learn how to move again and enjoy the pleasure of effort and the joys of a post-sport shower. I had the good luck to go into a small gymnasium in my village one day. I was welcomed with a big smile and outstretched hand, which helped me overcome my fears. I was gently encouraged to surpass my limits and, even though I had never played a sport in my life, I discovered its joys. If the first weeks were difficult, I quickly enjoyed the benefits. And "healthy eaters" will take comfort in the menus in which they, as new sportsmen, may now indulge. It goes without saying that if you want to lose weight without physical exercise, your menu will have to be frugal and your discipline severe. Whereas if you exercise, what a joy it is to watch, from week to week, your neglected body transformed, growing thinner and lighter, as it rediscovers a tone and dynamism that once seemed buried forever, a memory of childhood.

Do not champ at the bit. Do not be impatient. Allow yourself time to change your habits and forget the tyranny of the weighing machine. Measure your weight once a week; any more is unnecessary. Do not be too harsh on your body; give it time to find its balance.

Start by washing your hands. Long ago, I spent several months in Afghanistan, in the foothills of Pamir, at the heart of a small valley lined with olive trees and a meandering river. I took all my meals in a teahouse there. I would wear a suit and sit on a carpet spread on a large platform of plaited and stretched ropes tied to a wooden frame. Beneath, on the baked earth, chickens would peck at our crumbs. Before we were served a bowl of rice and lamb pilaf, with cinnamon and cloves, a young boy, eyes lined with kohl and hair all over the place, brought a copper bowl that he placed before us. In it was a small, delightfully fragrant Isfahan rose. It soon floated to the surface of the slightly warm water that the child poured from a large ewer. Then he placed the ewer next to the basin and passed us a fresh piece of embroidered linen to dry our hands.

In these crude surroundings, between the bare earth walls, the refinement of this purification ritual would plunge us daily into a Scheherazade tale, and it seemed to us that everybody who ate there,

In the red bedroom, fresh out of bed, a bowl of muesli and a glass of fresh fruit juice is ideal before going for a half-hour walk or run in the nearby countryside.

caravanners and truckers alike, must be enchanted princes. Above all, this ritual provided a calm, gentle moment before the meal. In the past, in many households, families gathered around the table would join hands to pray, thank God, and bless the food. This ritual, so different in its content to the other, had the same function or, in any case, the same effect.

At home, when I was a child, before each meal we would all participate in another delightful ritual—that of "setting the table." My mother would select the tablecloth and crockery. We would go into the garden and pick flowers, or red and yellow leaves in autumn. The positioning of the cutlery was essential; we learned that, in France, forks were placed facing downward to display the engraved figures and coats of arms on the back, while in England they faced upwards, so as not to scratch the mahogany of the table or snag in the lace of the napkins. Then came the moment to fold the serviettes, or drape them over the edge of plates with a natural air that was more elaborate than it appeared. In general, every day, the table was laid simply and cheerfully, but it was always carefully done. For celebrations, when my parents had guests in, the table settings were more sumptuous, and always very imaginative. This art reached its peak of perfection for meals in the garden, picnics, or snacks. There, our imagination knew no bounds, and we would find nothing more amusing than setting out china and silverware on a huge damask tablecloth spread on the grass beside the river bank. Through these unhurried, joyous activities, I have retained an unshakeable fondness for a well-set table.

Whatever they might be, all these rituals enable us to enter into the spirit of the meal before us. Eating quickly, without a second thought, while standing up or talking business, or even missing a meal, are all bad practices that only hinder finding the balance we seek. Be totally aware of what you eat, conscious of what you are doing, of chewing and swallowing, of the taste of things. Be aware of the pleasure of eating your fill, of talking about fine food at the dinner table, and of exchanging gastronomic memories. In all cases, avoid talking about things that annoy you; save conversations that are too serious or solemn for later. All this is indispensable for the art of living.

In the upstairs bedroom, a simple slice of wholemeal bread spread with peanut butter and a little honey, accompanied by a glass of fresh fruit juice or iced tea, along with a flower in a vase, provides all the energy and joy required for a whole morning.

ASPECTS OF
LIGHTER CUISINE

The best way to explain the principles involved in my approach is through practice. I have thus chosen several recipes that represent this new way of eating well. In explaining them, I have added comments to provide you with keys to lighter cuisine to help you avoid any pitfalls that might occur. In general, you should try to "lighten up" recipes as much as possible: use olive oil instead of butter, soy cream or low-fat yogurt to replace cream or crème fraîche. Try to keep amounts of lipids and carbohydrates to a minimum, but you need not eliminate them completely. You should also, in the same recipe, keep carbohydrates and fats separate, as you should animal proteins and carbohydrates. By regularly alternating foods rich in animal proteins with others where they are completely absent, you will quickly find an excellent nutritional balance. With a little practice, these constraints can be skirted around fairly easily to bring results that are always beneficial and often delicious.

The summer dining room opens onto the courtyard and garden,
sheltered from the mistral and the burning sun—the perfect place to enjoy
a delicious oven-baked sea bream.

Two *salades niçoises*

Traditionally, *salade niçoise* is a meal in itself. It contains raw vegetables, tomatoes, green peppers, and young white onions, as well as cooked vegetables, green beans, and potatoes. Proteins are provided by the canned tuna and anchovies and hard-boiled eggs. For seasoning, there are also black olives, olive oil and vinegar, salt, and pepper. However, the problem lies in the potatoes. These contain carbohydrates, which should not be eaten with fish and hard-boiled eggs. This difficulty has to be bypassed by preparing either a salad without potatoes or one without tuna, anchovies, and eggs. You can choose to eat one or the other, at lunch or dinnertime.

In the kitchen. For both salads, cut three nice firm, not-too-ripe summer tomatoes into quarters. Field-grown tomatoes, naturally cultivated and caressed daily by the sun, can be eaten almost green, as they have flavor come what may. (In contrast, greenhouse tomatoes, even when red, have no taste.) Arrange the tomatoes in a deep wide salad bowl. Add several fine strips of red pepper, and several rings cut from small green peppers with their seeds removed. You will need two young white onions, sliced into rounds, and some black olives.

Green beans lie on the interface between the two recipes, as they contain some sugars—not very many, but some nevertheless. If you want to be really strict, save the beans to accompany the potato salad. Choose ones that are young and without strings, top and tail them, and blanch them for several minutes in salted boiling water, uncovered, to keep their strong color. They should be cooked but firm. In a similar fashion, wash, peel, and cut several potatoes into thick slices, then cook them for about ten minutes in salted boiling water. Drain them, leave them to cool, then lay all the vegetables in the salad bowl. In this version, I like to add several small fresh fava beans with their thin outer skin removed, which I cook in boiling water for no more than three minutes. Decorate with several black Nice olives and there you have it.

Alternatively, boil as many eggs as you have guests. Run the eggs under cold water before peeling. Cut in two and lay them on the tomatoes. Open and drain a tin of plain tuna and crumble it coarsely. Wash several salted anchovies beneath cold running water and remove their tails, fins, and bones. Arrange them attractively on the salad with several black Nice olives.

For both salads, prepare a simple vinaigrette in a separate bowl with a little olive oil and very little wine vinegar, salt, and pepper. Serve this vinaigrette separately from the salad, which will allow you to season your salad lightly. Your guests can be more extravagant if they so wish.

Rice stuffed peppers

Stuffing vegetables or leaves is a common technique in all Mediterranean countries. Most often the stuffing is made of rice or bulgur wheat with chopped meat and varyious seasonings. The problem is, however, that our principle of keeping animal proteins separate from carbohydrates forbids us this combination. I am thus going to suggest two different recipes—one of peppers stuffed with rice and the other of tomatoes stuffed with meat. It is also possible to use both stuffings with eggplants, round zucchini, and mushrooms, as well as cabbage or vine leaves.

In the kitchen. Select good round peppers that are not too large, and allow two per person. Green peppers are a little more bitter than red peppers, which are more flavorsome. Yellow and orange peppers are the sweetest. Cut the tops from each pepper to form a lid, leaving the stalk attached. Remove the seeds and white ribs from inside. Wash 9 oz. (250 g) round rice, then pour into a saucepan and cover with two-and-a-half times its volume of water. Cook uncovered until the water has partly evaporated and it forms small craters on the surface of the rice. Turn off the heat and cover. The rice will finish swelling until you are ready to use it. Peel and finely chop one or two onions and fry them till golden in a little hot olive oil. In another pan, without oil, toast a soupspoon of pine nuts. This operation should be carried out over a low heat, taking care to stir the pine nuts constantly as they burn easily. Mix the onions and pine nuts with the juice of a lemon, two soupspoons of raisins, a good handful of frozen peas straight from the freezer, along with a pinch of cumin and fresh oregano, and salt and pepper. Fill the peppers with this stuffing. Put their lids on top and lay them in a gratin dish. Pour a glass of water into the bottom of the dish and cover with a sheet of aluminum foil so the rice does not burn. Then place the dish to cook in a hot oven for a good half-hour. Lower the heat to 300°F (150°C) and stew your peppers for a further twenty minutes or so. Remove them from the oven a quarter of an hour before serving and accompany with a small rocket or green-leaf salad.

Régis' little "nothing-to-it" soup

The fashion world, in its own ruthless and often hysterical way, is more obsessed by figure and diet than any other profession. Any weight gain, be it even half a pound, causes great trauma. Like all models, and also designers, publicists, and fashion assistants, my dear friend Régis is no exception to the rule. Unfortunately for him, he loves his food, and so he has to be doubly careful. But this has meant that he has been able to provide valuable dietary advice throughout the book and share this delicious soup recipe, which contains just seventeen calories per bowl!

In the kitchen. Carefully wash a large cucumber. Cut it into segments and place them in the bowl of a food processor together with eight small cartons of low fat yogurt, two soupspoons of olive oil, the leaves from two stalks of fresh mint, salt, and pepper. Blend together and chill. Just before serving, sprinkle with several leaves of finely chopped mint. For a delicious variation, replace the mint with coriander. And there you have a quick, fresh, and subtle starter that does not count in calories at all.

There really is "nothing to it"!

The big "everything-thrown-in" soup

Italian cookery is an inexhaustible source of inspiration, as it allies all the benefits of a Mediterranean diet and the simplicity of local flavoring to the refinement of an age-old art of living. This big, everything-thrown-in soup is minestrone, which combines fresh vegetables, dried beans and pulses, pasta or rice, and potatoes. There is not just one minestrone recipe; there are as many as there are chefs, and you too can invent your own. It is a marvelous dish in its own right for those days when it is cold outside.

In the kitchen. Soak 3$\frac{1}{2}$ oz. (100 g) of white haricot beans in a large salad bowl of cold water. The following day, in a large casserole dish, brown two finely chopped onions and two crushed cloves of garlic in a dash of olive oil over a gentle heat so that the garlic does not burn.

Add four peeled tomatoes, seeds removed and finely chopped, along with the drained beans. Then pour over 3 pints (2 liters) of cold water, add a pinch of fresh thyme leaves and one of fresh marjoram, and raise the heat. When it boils, lower the heat again and leave to simmer, covered, for two hours. Then add two carrots, two potatoes, and two peeled and diced turnips, and leave to cook for ten minutes. Add two finely sliced sticks of celery, 9 oz. (250 g) cabbage cut into strips, and a large handful of macaroni. Leave to simmer until the pasta is cooked. Add the chopped parsley, salt, and pepper. Pour it all into an attractive soup tureen and serve accompanied by a small bowl of grated pecorino cheese. I find Parmesan cheese too delicate for this rustic recipe. Whatever you use, consider the cheese as a seasoning, not as an ingredient.

China Sea salad

Here is a recipe for a delicious and flavorsome salad, with a remarkable seasoning that does not contain even a drop of oil. Wash and pick over a solid lettuce heart, several Chinese cabbage leaves, and a good handful of bean sprouts. Cut the lettuce and cabbage into strips, then lay them in a large salad bowl with the bean sprouts, 14 oz. (400 g) grated carrots, two scallions, their outer skin removed and finely chopped, and a good handful of coriander and mint leaves. If you use large winter carrots, peel then grate them; you need not grate young carrots. If the mint leaves are fleshy and a little tough, chop them finely before adding them to the salad; do not do this with small tender leaves. Steam twenty or so shrimps so that they retain their attractive pink color. Remove their heads and shells and lay them on the vegetables. The shrimps work well with crabmeat or finely sliced cold chicken with its skin removed. Pour over two soupspoons of *nuoc-mâm*, Vietnamese fish sauce, and two soupspoons of lime juice. Do not add salt as the *nuoc-mâm* is already very salty. Mix together well and serve immediately in individual small bowls, chopsticks at the ready!

Cardamom and cinnamon, ginger and mace, Sichuan pepper, mustard seeds, and tamarind, like so many other spices, on their own or blended with others, provide an extraordinary palette of savors and tastes, conferring intensity and style on the simplest of dishes.

Tomatoes stuffed with meat and *brousse* cheese

The remains of a meat stew or roast are ideal for this recipe. You will need three different meats: pork, lamb, and poultry. If you do not have any leftovers, grill two chicken breasts, a pork chop, and two slices from a leg of lamb. Season at the end of cooking and leave them to cool before removing their fat and bone. Chop them together fairly coarsely with two good-sized cloves of garlic, peeled and chopped. Peel and finely chop one or two onions and brown them in a pan with a little hot olive oil. Mix the chopped meats and garlic together in a salad bowl with the onions, two soup-spoons of raisins, a good pinch of fresh oregano leaves, and one of cinnamon. Add 5 oz. (150 g) of *brousse* cheese, or any fresh ewe's cheese, two whole eggs, and salt and pepper. Mix once more. Select ripe but firm round tomatoes. Cut them in two horizontally, remove their seeds and juice and fill them with the meat and cheese stuffing before arranging them in a gratin dish. Drizzle with olive oil and cook them for a good half-hour in a hot oven. Then lower the temperature of the oven to 300°F (150°C) and leave them to caramelize for another half an hour. Remove them from the oven a quarter of an hour before serving and accompany them with a small rocket or green-leaf salad.

Fromage-frais stuffed tomatoes

The tomatoes are served raw and are perfect as a cold starter, appetizer, or in a summer buffet. Choose small tomatoes. Cherry tomatoes are ideal, even if they require a little more care and patience. They should be ripe but not excessively so—that is to say, good and red but firm. Wash them and wipe carefully. Then cut a small lid from each and put on one side. Using a teaspoon, remove the seeds and juice from the tomatoes. In a salad bowl, mix 10 oz. (300 g) of fresh goat's cheese with salt, pepper, and chopped fresh herbs such as chives, mint, lemon balm, dill, or rocket. Fill each tomato with a spoonful of fromage frais and some of the cheese mixture, then replace their lids, using a cocktail stick to secure them. Arrange the tomatoes in a dish on a bed of fresh herbs or salad leaves. Cover the dish with kitchen wrap and keep in a cool place until you are ready to serve it.

You can follow this recipe to stuff small boat-shaped slices of de-seeded cucumber or celery, as well as mushroom caps.

Hummus and other Lebanese mezes

Lebanese mezes are feasts for the eye and palate. The table is covered in a multitude of dishes containing chickpeas and parsley, cucumber and tomato, tahini and pomegranate seeds, olive oil and lemon, in a symphony of sensual delight. The mezes are eaten slowly, in small mouthfuls. Guests taste a little of this and a little of that, crunching on a salad leaf in between. Some dishes are hot, others are served cold; all are delicious. One of the most famous is hummus, a purée of chickpeas and sesame paste. I always thought it was anything but low-calorie and so, in my great ignorance, I did not touch for a long time. In fact, so long as you do not eat more than your fill of these mezes and you do not have any animal protein or a sweet dish at the same meal, the six recipes that follow, and the bread that accompanies them, are perfectly compatible with our plan to live healthily and remain slim, making a totally harmonious meal for a summer lunch. Chickpeas, fried eggplants, and tahini are a little heavy for an evening meal.

In the kitchen. Wash 1¹/₂ lbs. (800 g) of chickpeas. You will need 14 oz. (400 g) for the hummus. The other half you will serve hot, whole, and flavored with cumin and garlic (see recipe page 44). Soak the chick peas in 3 pints (2 liters) cold water for 24 hours with a teaspoon of bicarbonate of soda. The following day, pour away the soaking water and place the soaked peas in 5 pints (3 liters) cold water in a large saucepan. Bring to a boil, lower the heat, cover, and leave to simmer until the chickpeas are tender, skimming regularly to remove the skins that rise to the surface. They will take about forty-five minutes. Save several ladles of cooking liquid before straining the chickpeas. Remove half the chickpeas and purée in a vegetable mill over a wide dish (do not blend them, as it will turn this delicious dish into wallpaper paste). Add eight soupspoons of sesame paste to the purée; this can be found in Eastern and organic grocery stores, and is known as "tahini." In a mortar, crush three or four cloves of garlic with two pinches of coarse salt. Add the juice of four lemons and blend them into the purée until they are all smooth and creamy. If necessary, add one or two spoons of water to help you reach this texture. Serve the hummus in a small dish drizzled with a little olive oil.

Four meze recipes, from left to right:
Chickpeas with cumin (recipe page 44), tabbouleh (recipe page 42),
hummus, and eggplants in pomegranate juice (recipes page 42).

Tabbouleh

In a sieve, rinse 5 oz. (150 g) of cracked wheat, otherwise known as bulgur wheat in Turkey or "bourghol" in Lebanon. Leave it to soak for at least half an hour so that it swells. Wash six fresh, bushy bunches of flat parsley, as well as two bunches of mint leaves, and drain them carefully. Remove the leaves from the parsley and mint, throw away the stalks, and chop the leaves. Place two large tomatoes in boiling water, then into cold water. Peel and dice them and squeeze in your hand to remove the seeds. Finely chop two white onions and sprinkle with salt and pepper. Mix everything in a large salad bowl and season with lemon juice and olive oil. Adjust the seasoning. Cover with plastic wrap and place in the refrigerator for half an hour. Serve the tabbouleh and hummus, Arabian salad, chickpeas in cumin, and eggplants in pomegranate juice at the same time around a large plate of raw vegetables, salad leaves, and herbs. Your guests can dip these in the hummus or nibble them in between slices of eggplant.

Eggplants in pomegranate juice

Peel 2¼ lbs. (1 kg) of long, firm eggplants and cut them into ½-inch (1-cm) thick slices along their length. Sprinkle the slices generously with salt and leave to rest for at least an hour, then squeeze them between your hands to extract the juice. Fry them in a pan, in very hot olive oil; as soon as they take on a good bronze color, remove using a skimming ladle. Lay them on kitchen paper in a large dish tilted at a slight incline to allow the excess oil to drain. Cut a pomegranate in two and, using a lemon squeezer, extract its juice; or, better still, use a grape press. It is not a good idea to use an electric juicer, as it is too vigorous and may crush the pomegranate seeds, giving your juice an unpleasant flavor. Remove the seeds from the other half of the fruit, taking off all the little pieces of white skin in between. Arrange the fried eggplants in a dish, sprinkle with pomegranate seeds, and pour over the juice.

A large plate of raw vegetables

Such a dish always appears on Middle-Eastern tables, whatever is on the menu. It includes several lemon quarters, crisp leaves of Romaine lettuce, small lettuce hearts, leaves from a white cabbage heart, tomatoes, sticks of peeled cucumber with their seeds removed, fresh fava beans, scallions, radishes, a handful of purslane and another of rocket, or a bunch of flat leaf parsley, coriander, or mint. Depending on the accompanying menu, you may also add carrots cut into small sticks, celery stalks, white or red endive leaves, slices of black radish, soybean sprouts, small florets of cauliflower and even, perhaps, nasturtium flowers. The raw vegetable plate adds a delicious fresh touch to any highly flavorsome, aromatic meal. Here it is perfect with our mezes, but I do recommend that you make up a plate of raw vegetables and herbs on these lines as often as possible; this could accompany many other dishes with which a dressed salad would prove too extravagant and rich in oil.

Vegetables are rich in fiber, not to mention variety, taste, color and texture.
They as indispensable for vegetarian meals as they are to accompany meat and fish.

Chickpeas with cumin

Crush three cloves of garlic with a little coarse salt. Transfer to a small salad bowl. Add the remaining half of the chickpeas cooked for the hummus, with several soupspoons of their cooking water. Sprinkle with a handful of chopped parsley, a teaspoon of cumin and, if you feel like it, a small pinch of chili powder. Drizzle with a little olive oil and mix well. This chickpea salad can be served hot, but it is equally delicious when cooled.

Arabian salad

Wash and pick over a nice crisp Romaine lettuce and cut it into thin strips. In a salad bowl, crush a clove of garlic with a little coarse salt, add the juice of half a lemon, two small sliced scallions, a large handful of chopped parsley, and a smaller one of mint leaves. Pour several soupspoons of olive oil over the herbs and garlic and mix well. Be careful not to toss the salad in this mixture until the last minute, just before serving.

Roast pan chicken

Whether you prepare chicken or guinea fowl for this recipe, you need to use free-range, grain-fed, sustainably farmed or organic poultry—not to be confused with farm poultry raised, despite its name, in a battery. As always the quality of the produce is essential and the only guarantee of the result, especially when the preparation is simple.

In the kitchen. Have your butcher clean out and tie up a good-sized grain-fed chicken, without barding, as this adds nothing. Heat the oven to 400°F (200°C). Place the chicken in the middle of a heavy-based, cast-iron, oval casserole dish, and surround it with twenty or so garlic cloves in their skins. Place the lid on the casserole dish and place it in the middle of your oven for an hour. There is nothing more to it.

This cooking method avoids filling your oven with spitting oil, and so does not fill the kitchen with clouds of pungent, burning-fat smoke. Above all, you will be surprised, as I was, by the chicken's attractive, crispy golden skin, by the tenderness of the meat, and by its perfect flavor even in the absence of salt and spices. And as for the cloves of garlic cooked in chicken juice—sublime!

Carpaccio

It was to satisfy the dietary requirements of an elegant habitué of Harry's Bar in Venice that the chef of the famous restaurant invented this recipe and named it "carpaccio," after the great Venetian painter of the fifteenth century. The doctor had prescribed "raw beef." So a fillet of beef was cut in the same manner as Parma ham was in Italy at that time, in wafer-thin, translucent slices that were simply seasoned with fillets of anchovies and capers in vinegar. Since that moment, this recipe has met with considerable worldwide success, and today carpaccios are made from and with everything, and are often bathed in olive oil and piled with artichokes, tomatoes, lemon quarters, and slices of Parmesan. Restaurateurs freeze beef to create a solid block that can then be machine-cut into such thin sections. At home, where ham-slicing machines are not common, the Harry's Bar method is preferred.

In the kitchen. Cut fine, ¼-inch (5-mm) slices from a fillet of beef, working across, not against, the grain of the meat. Spread two sheets of plastic wrap on the table and brush them carefully with a little excellent-quality olive oil. Lay your slices of beef between the oiled sides of the two sheets, spacing them out with room to spare. Using a wooden beater, gently and evenly flatten the meat. It will spread easily, and soon you will be able to see light through it. Remove the first layer of plastic and flip the meat over onto a large plate. You can then remove the top sheet. The olive oil brushed on the meat will have been absorbed and given it sufficient flavor, so there is no need to add extra. There is no need to add extra salt either if you dress the carpaccio with salted anchovy fillets. Remove their bones carefully under cold running water and arrange them on the meat. Sprinkle with capers to bring a necessary touch of tartness. In this way, you will not need to add lemon, which would immediately cook the meat. Add a few chopped chives for color, chopped onion for delicate flavor, and ground pepper. You can serve this outrageously simple dish straight away, accompanied by a small rocket salad with olive oil and lemon.

Penne à la puttanesca

Here is another Italian recipe that I learned in Mykonos in Greece, thirty years ago, in the company of my friend Piero Aversa, as, oozing blue paintbrushes in hand, we added the final touches to the door and shutters of his bar, "Piero's." The bar quickly became a great favorite of the seventies' jet set. *Penne à la puttanesca* was the only hot dish that Piero would cook on demand, at any hour of the night, and sometimes in the early hours of the morning, to revitalize weary clients after hours of frenzied disco-dancing. There is nothing easier, especially if your cupboard is regularly stocked; all the ingredients should be there. It is perfect as a last-minute improvisation.

In the kitchen. Start by heating a large pan of hot water. You can never cook pasta in too much water. While the water is heating, and in a pan, fry two onions and two chopped cloves of garlic on a gentle heat until golden. If you have a red pepper at hand, dice it after removing the stalk, seeds, and white ribs, and add to the pan. If you do not, no matter: the pepper is optional. Break up one or two small red chili peppers and add them. Then pour in 1 lb. ($^1/_2$ kg) peeled and chopped canned tomatoes and raise the heat, stirring regularly to help the sauce reduce. This last operation should not take more than five minutes. Turn off the heat and add three finely chopped cloves of garlic, which will not cook, to the sauce, and a small glass of drained capers in vinegar. Meanxhile, when the water boils in the pan, add a handful of coarse salt and pour in the pasta. This should cook the minimum time indicated on the packet, as it has to be *al dente*. When the pasta has cooked, pour a ladle of its cooking water into a large salad bowl before draining. Then pour the drained pasta into the salad bowl and cover it with the tomato sauce, mix, and serve piping hot. Serve yourself seconds of pasta rather than leading yourself astray with a dessert. Grated cheese is not really permitted, but I never can resist the pleasure of a light sprinkling. With a tomato sauce as fully flavored as the *puttanesca*, Parmesan is probably too delicate, so I prefer Pecorino cheese. Of course, for all recipes in this book, do not buy pre-wrapped cheese, and make sure you grate it yourself. Above all, ignore that gruesome grated Parmesan you find in sachets.

Sandra's huge fish

My friend Sandra is a fairy, I am convinced. I have several times seen her very clearly on certain summer evenings at the instant the sun gives way to the moon, and her pearl-dappled wings flutter on her back and shimmer. The only thing that makes me doubt my belief is her passion for cookery because, as I understand it, fairies only need dewdrops for nourishment.

When it comes to cooking fish, the simplest methods are the best. And the most simple is definitely to do as my friend Sandra does.

In the kitchen. For this very easy recipe, you will need a large, very fresh fish. You might choose a nice sea bream, or sea bass, or a small bonito, as even small bonitos are a good size.

Have your fish-seller gut the fish but ask him not to remove the scales. Wipe with kitchen paper inside and out. Heat the oven to 400°F (200°C). Fill your oven broiling pan with an inch of hot water and replace it in the upper part of the oven. Lay your fish on a grill pan and place it two inches above the surface of the water. Close your oven and allow half an hour cooking time for a 4 lb. (2 kg) fish. When cooked, slide the fish onto a serving dish and remove the skin, which will lift off easily with all its scales. Serve immediately with coarse sea salt and lemon quarters, a mixed green-leaf salad and a cucumber *raita*, or a "little sauce that makes all the difference" (see recipe page 135). This light dish is perfect for dinner.

Blanquette of veal with leeks and chicken casserole with vegetables

Blanquette of veal is a dish that is too rich. But prepared this way where leeks are used to flavor the sauce and to replace the rice or potatoes that accompany the meat, it can be a marvel of lightness and delicacy. What's more, you can use soy cream, the marvelous, low-fat, vegetable-based substitute with its neutral flavor, to replace the cream or crème fraîche and make the sauce white and creamy.

In the kitchen. Start by blanching the veal. Cut 2 lbs. (1 kg) meat from the shank, breast, or shoulder into egg-sized pieces. Lay them in a large pan and cover with cold water. Bring the water to the boil and, as soon as it boils, pour the contents of the pan through a strainer. Rinse the pieces of meat in lots of cold water to wash out any elements that could cloud the cooking stock. Replace the pieces of meat in the pan and cover with 5 pints (3 liters) cold water. Add a little salt, a peeled carrot, and a whole onion with three cloves pressed into it, a piece of mace, the outer husk of a nutmeg, a piece of dry orange peel, and a bouquet garni made of carefully washed leek leaves, parsley, a stick of celery, two bay leaves, and a small sprig of thyme, all firmly tied together. Cover and allow to simmer for an hour and a half. During this time, pick through and carefully wash 4 lbs. (2 kg) leeks and cut off any greenery. Cut the leeks into segments of the same length and tie them together in a bundle using two lengths of string. After an hour of cooking, add the bundle of leeks to the pan, cover again, and leave to cook for half an hour. In a bowl, thoroughly mix together a teaspoon of cornstarch, three egg yolks, and 8 fl. oz. (250 ml) of soy cream. Place this mixture in a saucepan and pour over a ladle of hot stock, whisking constantly. Return the pan to a gentle heat and add a second ladle of stock, then a third, stirring continuously. Be careful not to reach boiling point so that the egg yolks do not solidify and form lumps. Add another pinch of grated nutmeg, the juice of half a lemon, and ground pepper. Generally I prefer adding the pepper at the last moment, as it has more flavor when it is not cooked. One final hint: a little grated truffle at the last moment does no damage to the delicate flavor of the sauce.

Remove the pieces of meat using a skimming ladle, and lay them on one side of a hot dish. Drain the bundle of leeks for a moment or two before laying it next to the meat. Remove the string. Coat the veal in several spoonfuls of the creamy sauce and serve immediately with the rest of the sauce in a sauceboat.

And one further, final remark. Chicken casserole can be prepared in exactly the same way. However, as you will not have to blanch the chicken, miss out the first stage of the recipe. Chose a good free-range chicken and replace the leek with quarters of celeriac and carrots.

Cheese and dessert

If only it was possible to go without…. If it is not, you will already have gathered that you have a choice to make, depending both on what the dessert of your heart's desire would be (to which I strongly advise you to pay heed), and also on the composition of your menu. If your meal has been light, featuring poultry or fish and green vegetables, then you can add cheese to the menu. Go for fresh goat's- or ewe's-milk cheeses rather than a rich creamy Brie or a hard goat's cheese marinated in olive oil. Take your cheese with a mixed green-leaf salad to avoid eating bread. If your meal was vegan, however, continue in the same vein and skip cheese. Tuck into a few strawberries instead, or some other seasonal fruit at its ripest, to avoid having to add sugar. At the end of the book, I have devoted a chapter to desserts, but please do not read it straight away….

Old-fashioned hot chocolate

I do not want to get your hopes up; chocolate is not one of the principles of this healthy living plan. However, encouraging pleasure and keeping frustration at bay are necessary for its success. Here, then, for chocoholics, is a time-honored way of preparing a cup of dark, slightly bitter yet creamy hot chocolate, for snack times. You will need 1 oz. (30 g) chocolate per cup from an eighty-five percent cocoa bar. The sweetness is strangely much more obvious to the palate in melted chocolate than when solid. Break the chocolate into pieces and melt it into as many cups of water as you wish to serve, in a heavy-based pan, stirring constantly with a whisk. Whisking is indispensable for the creaminess of the drink, as chocolate has a tendency to form lumps in contact with water. You should be careful not to boil the chocolate so as not to alter its flavor. It is said that chocolate should never be heated above a temperature of 120°F (50°C). When the chocolate has melted and the liquid starts to steam gently, but before it boils, whisk it well and keep whisking, then pour your hot chocolate into a pot and serve immediately.

EGGS, MEAT AND FISH, YOGURT AND CHEESE

For a long time rare, red meat has been associated with virile physiques and warrior virtues. The theory goes that consumption of large quantities of animal proteins helps build muscles and melt away fat. This idea is partially correct, or not completely false. However, it was once so firmly anchored in our consciousness or sub-consciousness that a host of protein powders and food substitutes appeared on the market and were instantly successful. I refuse here even to pass comment on such evil-looking floury substances. In contrast, when I think about cooking eggs, meat, fish, or dairy produce (all foods containing animal protein) I feel excited: all my signals start flashing, my eyes glow, and my taste buds salivate. Nevertheless, cooking this type of food requires some precautions from the health point of view. Egg yolks, for example, which are an excellent source of protein, are very high in cholesterol and should be consumed in moderation. The same goes for red meats like beef and lamb. Choose white meats instead, above all poultry, and avoid eating the skin, even if it is golden and crunchy. Cooked animal fats like pork or beef fat should be avoided completely. This is why you should use cooking methods that do not add fat to fat, like steaming, or baking in paper parcels. However, there is no restriction on fresh fish. Even fatty fish like tuna, mackerel, sardines, and salmon can be recommended. As for milk products, it is fine to have fat-free yogurt at your table nearly every day, but cheese is too rich for frequent consumption, except for fresh goat and ewe cheeses.

Quails' eggs, prawns, and shiitake mushrooms are the "three treasures" of Madam Ong's soup (recipe page 69).

Goat cheese stuffed zucchini flowers

This recipe is very similar to the one for stuffed sardines (see recipe page 61). The difficulty will no doubt come in finding fresh zucchini flowers if you live in a cool temperate climate. Allow three flowers per person and remove the stalks and peduncle. Prepare the stuffing with fresh creamy goat cheese (a soupspoon per flower) into which you incorporate a beaten egg, chopped chives, salt, and pepper. You can also simply use plain goat cheese, without any additions; the dish is quicker to make and just as delicious. Fill each flower with the stuffing and flatten them out slightly. Brown quickly in a pan in a small dash of olive oil and serve as a starter.

Greek salad

Horiatiko salata is a dish that working Greeks eat every day. This Greek salad combines ripe, firm, peeled, deseeded, diced tomatoes with cucumbers that have first been peeled and sliced in two lengthways, then cut into half-inch (1 cm) thick slices. Then come strips of young green, peeled, deseeded peppers, sliced rounds of sweet onion, a good slab of feta, the goat's cheese that is conserved in salt water then drained, and several black olives. The Greeks have two traditional vinaigrettes. One combines two measures of olive oil with a measure of vinegar, salt, pepper, fresh oregano, and chopped parsley. We will use this to season our Greek salad before serving. In the other, lemon juice replaces vinegar in the same proportions and is served with boiled vegetables like green beans, zucchini, artichokes, or cauliflowers.

The combination of feta, cucumber, tomato, and olives is so good that I often serve cubes of feta, sticks of cucumber, cherry tomatoes, and black Greek olives without seasoning as an appetizer. In this case I do not serve a starter and go straight onto the main course.

Beef tartare and tomato tartare

When I was a child growing up in France in the fifties, steak tartare was called "American steak" in homage to the liberation army, and it featured on the menus of all respectable restaurants at that time, next to turbot with hollandaise sauce and peach melba. The dish consisted of a peculiar mixture of raw chopped beef, capers, dill pickles, parsley, and shallots, drowned in a strange sauce composed of exotic substances such as tomato ketchup and Worcester sauce, dashes of innumerable bottles of various colors, all bound together with an egg yolk. It was invariably served with fries. The raw beef was barely discernible, hidden behind its thick mask. There was very little "tartare" involved, a word that to me has more to do with rough living and frugality, and with raw meat ground beneath the saddles of Central Asian horsemen. The version I propose here is much more refined, and is accompanied, as an echo or a reflection, by a very fresh tomato tartare.

In the kitchen. For the beef tartare, you will need 4 oz. (125 g) of lean sirloin or rump steak per person. Remove all skin and fat from the meat, then cut it into slices and chop it finely with a knife. Chop a handful of rocket and the flesh of half a cucumber, peeled with its seeds removed. Place all the ingredients in a terrine and mix with a dash of olive oil, salt, and pepper. The cucumber brings unique freshness to the dish while the rocket brings flavor, enhanced by the pepper.

For the tomato tartare, you will need one or two nice firm tomatoes that you should place first in boiling water, then cold; this will enable you to peel them easily. Cut them in two and remove the seeds, then dice very small. Add one scallion, finely sliced into rounds, a good handful of flat chopped parsley, a thin drizzle of olive oil, and a dash of Worcester sauce. Add salt, pepper, and mix together. Serve the two tartares at the same time, surrounded by small fresh, plump, crispy lettuce hearts.

Scorpion fish salad with cherries

There is always a point in the month of June when the cherry boughs sag beneath the weight of their fruit and it is hard to know what to do with all of it. To begin with, it is a good idea to climb into the trees and feast heartily, perched in the branches, until you can eat no more. Then, it is time to make a *clafoutis*, a traditional fruit dessert made with a sweet batter, a dish that can also be made in a low-calorie version (see recipe page 131). From then on, it is time to invent. The inspiration for this recipe came when I was preparing a Tahitian fish dish with raw fish marinated in lemon juice, where the lemon's acidity gently "cooks" the fish.

In the kitchen. Squeeze the juice from seven or eight lemons into a salad bowl. Cut several fresh fillets of scorpion fish into strips, allowing 5 oz. (150 g) fish per person. Place them in the lemon juice. Add a pound of large red, almost black, firm, crunchy cherries that have been cut in two and pitted. The juice from the cherries will seep into the marinade and make it flush with joy. Cover in plastic wrap and refrigerate for two hours. Just before serving, sprinkle with finely sliced rounds of scallion and several coriander and mint leaves, a little salt, and a good dose of pepper. The dish is then ready. And why not take this surprising salad into the garden for a picnic beneath the cherry trees?

Stuffed sardines with *brousse* cheese from the Rove hills

Brousse du Rove is a mythical Provençal cheese, soft and creamy made from the milk of the large russet goats, with their superb horns, raised on the hills behind Marseilles. If this cheese is not available, any fresh goat's or ewe's cheese or cottage cheese is perfectly suitable for this recipe.

In the kitchen. Choose good, hard, shimmering, fresh sardines. You will need at least four per person and always an even number. Beneath gently running cold water, use your thumbs to scale the sardines without damaging the skin. Then, with a pair of scissors, cut off their heads, open them in half, and gut them. Then, remove their backbones without cutting off their tails. They are now open and flat.

Prepare the stuffing with the cheese (you will need two soupspoons for each pair of sardines) into which you should incorporate one or two eggs, depending on their size and the quantity of cheese used, salt, and pepper—and that is all.

Onto one open sardine put $1/2$ inch (1 cm) of stuffing, and cover with the other sardine, like a sandwich, the skin toward the outside. Arrange the stuffed sardines in a gratin dish, which should be lightly coated with olive oil. Brush them with a little more olive oil and cook in the oven for about twenty minutes until golden. There you go. They are delicious straight from the oven accompanied by a mixed green-leaf salad seasoned with olive oil and ginger...and, of course, friends!

Squash and prawn soup with Sichuan pepper

Sichuan pepper, traditionally used in the Chinese province of that name, is one of the latest spices to arrive in the West. It is one of the ingredients of Chinese five-spice, along with cinnamon, cloves, fennel seeds, and star anise. Used on its own, however, it has a surprisingly powerful aroma that is acrid, hot, and lemony, with undertones of flowers and mint. It completely transforms this squash soup and combines perfectly with Mediterranean prawns.

In the kitchen. Boil 3 pints (2 liters) of slightly salted water. Remove the skin and seeds of a good 2^1/$_4$-lb. (1-kg) slice of squash. Cut it into chunks and cook them for about three-quarters of an hour on a low heat. While the squash is cooking, shell several good-sized prawns, two per person, or several large shrimps, in which case you will need more. Cut the prawns into inch-long (2-cm) sections or, if you are using shrimps, leave them whole. When the squash is ready (when a fork slips readily into the flesh), remove the pan from the heat and blend the soup. Several minutes before serving, return the soup to the heat and, when it starts boiling, add the prawns and cook for a further two minutes, just long enough for them to turn a good pink color, then turn off the heat. Add more salt if necessary. Divide the soup between individual bowls and share out the prawns. Add a dash of soy cream to each bowl and sprinkle the surface with several grains of Sichuan pepper. I like to follow this delightful starter with a salmon roasted *en papillote*, served with a spinach curry (see recipes page 70 and page 105).

Tadeusz' iced soup

Tadeusz was a Pole. His smile had more shining presence in his eyes than on his mouth, and his warm voice was nicely rounded by his beautiful Central European accent. His artistic hands could achieve anything, so alike are cookery and painting. We often prepare this iced red beet soup, with its unlikely pink color and fresh gentle flavor, and it delights us every time.

In the kitchen. Peel 3^1/$_2$ lbs. (1^1/$_2$ kg) of raw red beets. Dice them and cook them in 3 pints (2 liters) salted water. All the color from the red beet should pass into the stock. You should cook them until the water is very red and the cubes of red beet seem to lose their color. When you reach this stage, strain into a soup tureen, throw away the red beet and allow the soup to cool. Cover in plastic wrap and keep cool. In Poland, people then add a ladle of soured cream that has fermented like yogurt. It is delicious but far too rich for our purposes. So, before serving, mix two low-fat yogurts into the red beet soup, add a finely grated cucumber and a handful of finely chopped dill and chives. Tadeusz also used to float several attractive half-moons of boiled egg on the surface of the soup.

Lan's *phô* soup

The recipe for this delicious soup takes us to faraway ancient Tonkin, where silver rivers curl into the mist, and where squat mountains, neatly aligned like scales on a dragon's back, hide mysterious, fragrant pagodas in the folds of their cloak-like clouds. Because of this recipe, I nearly fell out with my friend Lan. Lan Huong Pham is an expert in Asian art. With her tales of warriors and concubines through long successions of dynasties, she led me along the Silk Roads. My knowledge of Chinese antiquities extended no farther than the large decorated porcelain jars that feature in Tintin's adventure in China, *The Blue Lotus*. Lan showed me the beauty of the patina of bronze statues, the soft skin of powdered clay, and the pale depths of ceramic glaze. And then, during a celebration, she treated us to her boiling *phô* soup of rice noodles, meat, herbs, and stock. However, when I suggested I feature the recipe here, adding flippantly that I would replace the rice noodles to produce a perfect healthy recipe, she fiercely opposed such a sacrilegious omission. Here, then, is the complete recipe.

In the kitchen. Remove the outer layer of an onion. Place it on its own in a hot oven and let it cook for half an hour so that it takes on a good dark caramel color.

Boil 5 pints (3 liters) of water in a pan. Add a marrowbone, 10 oz. (300 g) short rib beef, several spare ribs of pork, and a chicken carcass. Wait for the water to boil before lowering the heat. Add a piece of fresh, peeled, coarse-cut ginger, five or six star anise, two sticks of cinnamon, and the rich amber oven-baked onion skin.

Season very sparingly with salt and several peppercorns. Do not forget when seasoning that later we will be adding the highly salted Vietnamese fish sauce, *nuoc-mâm*. Lower the heat, cover, and leave to cook on a very slow boil for two hours, skimming the surface from time to time. Strain the stock and keep warm.

To serve the *phô*, you will need large porcelain bowls. In each bowl, place a small handful of rice noodles that have been boiled, rinsed with cold water, and carefully drained. (Of course, when it comes to eating lighter, you can leave out the noodles and replace them with bean sprouts.) Into each bowl, share out 10 oz. (300 g) of raw beef fillet cut into strips as for a carpaccio. Add chopped chives and three finely sliced scallions, then drown with boiling broth to cook the meat. On the table, in as many bowls, lay out bean sprouts, mint leaves, coriander, Asian basil, quarters of lime, and chopped chilis, not forgetting a bottle of *nuoc-mâm* so that everybody can season and flavor their soup as they wish. The Vietnamese add a herb they call *ngo gaï*, which may be translated as "thorn herb." It is readily available in Asian grocery stores. Do try it: it adds a delicious and authentic flavor to this soup, and its delicate aroma combines marvelously with the subtle combination of cinnamon, star anise, and mint. Serve the *phô* with chopsticks and porcelain spoons.

The soup makes a meal in its own right for any dinner occasion. Its abundance of vegetables enlivens the dinner table and will provide your guests with a delicious and filling meal. For dessert, serve a sorbet with fine slices of crystallized ginger. But be careful of the ginger: it bites.

*R*aita, *talattouri,* and yogurt dressing

Yogurt features strongly in the cuisines of the Near and Middle East, and of India: on its own, flavored, spiced, mixed with herbs, cucumber, or fruit, served as a sauce for dipping bread, as an accompaniment to rice dishes, roast meats, or meat sauces, or as a balm to calm the fire of a curry. It is even turned into a lightly salted drink, *ayran* in Turkey and *lassi* in India.

Raita is a refreshing sauce that accompanies all spiced dishes in northern India. To prepare it, pour two pots of low-fat yogurt into a bowl and beat to make them liquid. Into another bowl place a finely sliced sweet onion as well as a small green chili with its seeds removed. Add chopped mint and coriander. Season and mix together before pouring in the yogurt. Cover in plastic wrap and leave to rest for two hours in the refrigerator. Then mix once more before serving. In Madras, finely grated fresh coconut flesh is added to the sauce, and it is even more delicious.

The yogurt-cucumber combination is the most obvious and most widespread. In Cyprus, it is called *talattouri*. It is made with drained ewe's yogurt and so is thick. The peeled cucumber is cut in four, then finely sliced. It is then mixed with yogurt, a little garlic, chopped mint, a soupspoon of fruity olive oil, and a little salt. *Talattouri* is served in a meze or to accompany crudités and fish.

Traditional fresh and light recipes like these inspire dieticians today. It spells real progress to replace oil with low-fat yogurt in a salad dressing. While I was wrapped up in my obsession about losing weight, my friend Kathryn, a tall, attractive American, one of those women who will always be slender whatever she does or eats, came to the house, glowing and triumphant, carrying a Tupperware box in her hands, as though it was the Holy Grail. The box contained "yogurt dressing," a cornerstone of a healthy living plan. We tasted it and it was perfect. She then solemnly revealed the formula to me. She had copied it in full from a magazine, and I am reproducing it here. It consists of mixing two soupspoons of chopped chives with two non-fat yogurts, salt, and pepper. You can develop this recipe according to taste, with other herbs, spices, lemon, garlic, or onion. I am sure Kathryn would not be offended. Present this sauce in a bowl next to the salad. Help yourself to crudités and cover them in yogurt dressing. I assure you, the result is amazing!

Fish tartare

The Japanese have developed a subtle art with raw fish, working it in infinite combinations of *sashimis* and *sushis*. *Sashimis* are simply pieces of fresh fish, elegantly cut into bite-sized pieces, and served as they come, raw, without seasoning. In this way you can really appreciate the differences in flavor between tuna, salmon, and sea bream, for example. *Sushis* are small pieces of raw fish, wrapped in cooked, round-grained rice, eaten cold, very lightly seasoned with sugar and rice vinegar. The vinegar has an almost redundant flavor that brings out that of the fish. *Sushis* and *sashimis* are traditionally served with fine shavings of ginger marinated in vinegar and a touch of a very fiery green mustard, called *wasabi*, both of which are used to stimulate the palate in between mouthfuls of fish. Tahitians, however, serve raw fish that has marinated for several hours in lime juice (see recipe page 61). Our tartare recipes are inspired by these two traditions. Salmon, tuna, mackerel, and scallops will be served raw without a marinade so as to respect the fullness of their flavors, but they will be sufficiently seasoned so as not to surprise our Western palates too much.

In the kitchen. Have your fishmonger fillet two fresh mackerel for you. You also need a fillet, or two slices, of wild salmon. Avoid farmed salmon for this recipe. You will also need a slab of red tuna and six or eight scallops. In all, you should have 4 oz. (120 g) of fish per person.

At home, remove the skin of the salmon and tuna, leaving the mackerel skin on. Remove any bones using tweezers. Cut the salmon flesh, tuna, and scallops into strips, and chop each fish separately with a knife. As mackerel flesh is softer, it just pulls apart with a knife, then you chop it. Place the raw fish into four bowls, one for each type.

To the tuna flesh, add a dash of olive oil, a good handful of chopped parsley, and chives, ground pepper, and a pinch of coarse sea salt. Mix together.

To the salmon flesh, add a squeeze of lime juice, several drops of sesame oil (be careful: this oil has a strong flavor), several thin round slices of scallions, coarse sea salt, and ground pepper. Mix together.

To the mackerel flesh, add a large handful of rocket cut into strips, a finely chopped shallot, a squeeze of lemon juice, coarse sea salt, and ground pepper. Mix together.

Finally, for the scallops, to a very small dash of lemon juice add a teaspoon of lavender honey, salt, and pepper. Mix together, then pour this over the tartare.

Serve immediately with a mixed green salad of fairly thick leaves such as purslane or young spinach shoots, or even endives.

The flesh of any fish that is not bony can be prepared in this way. Have fun experimenting with new recipes using other seasonings, herbs, oils, and condiments, like mint and coriander,

Madam Ong's "three treasure soup"

Saigon still bore some scars from the war. The streets were full of potholes and rolls of barbed wire garlanded the tops of walls. However, the city's teeming life was beginning to take over once more. Maddening crowds of bicycles were evrywhere and large concrete buildings built to a strange, neo-Greek design had started appearing. In the middle of this imbroglio was hidden a small, tranquil house, shrouded in mystery and surrounded by a tiny lawn that an old gardener, squatting on his heels, constantly clipped with a pair of scissors. In the kitchen reigned the diminutive Madam Ong. To begin with, I was not allowed to enter. But via my repeated smiling and highly merited compliments of her excellent dishes, Madam Ong became my friend, and I was finally able to glimpse one or two of her secrets. Here is the recipe for her sublime "three treasure soup."

In the kitchen. Prepare a chicken stock by cooking two chicken carcasses in 5 pints (3 liters) of water for two hours, along with a piece of ginger, two sticks of Chinese cinnamon, and one star anise. Meanwhile, remove the heads and shells of twenty or so large shrimps, leaving the ends of their tails. Then split each shrimp in two lengthways. This way, when they are cooking later on, they will curl into delightful shapes like ram's horns. Allow twenty or so quails' eggs to hard boil for six minutes. Then run them under cold water before delicately removing their shells. Prepare twenty or so shiitake mushrooms; these can easily be found in grocery stores. Remove the stalks from the caps and add the stalks to the stockpot. Cut the caps into strips or leave them whole. Here we have our "three treasures." Cut several leaves of Chinese cabbage into strips and remove the leaves from several stalks of coriander. Strain the stock into another pan and replace it on a low heat. Add the shrimp tails and mushroom caps. Allow to cook for three minutes. In individual bowls, lay the quails' eggs, shrimps, and mushrooms on a bed of finely chopped Chinese cabbage, then pour on the boiling stock, seasoned simply with several drops of *nuoc-mâm*, and decorate with several coriander leaves. You will need chopsticks and porcelain spoons to eat this soup.

Roast salmon *en papillote*

Cooking fish *en papillote* is an excellent method. Underneath the shell of paper, the fish cook in the steam of their own juices, flavored by the herbs and condiments that surround them. All the cooking aromas are retained, which prevents fishy smells escaping into the house, and it makes the moment when the paper parcel is pierced and the fragrant steam suddenly bursts forth all the more intense. Many firm-fleshed fish lend themselves well to this mode of cooking, and in particularly oily fish like mackerel, tuna, and salmon. I wrap mackerel up with rounds of onion and slices of fresh ginger; serve tuna on a bed of lemon slices; and salmon as described in the recipe that follows here.

In the kitchen. Have your fishmonger cut you a large slab of salmon with the skin, from the middle of the body. Wrap this in a large sheet of aluminum or waxed cooking paper, folding up the edges up carefully so that nothing escapes from the parcel. Aluminum foil is very practical, but waxed cooking paper or parchment paper, which browns slightly during cooking, is to my mind more attractive. The choice is yours. This is all you will need. No olive oil, salt, herbs, or anything. Lay the wrapped salmon in the middle of an oven dish and place the dish in a very hot oven for half an hour. Ideally the fish should still be almost raw at the bone. However, it should fall away from the bone easily. Cooking for longer dries the fish out and this would be a shame. Serve directly from oven to table and open the *papillote* in front of your guests. They can add pepper and coarse sea salt according to taste. As an accompaniment, a spinach curry with cloves (see recipe page 105) and a cucumber *raita* (see page 65) are ideal.

Sea bream from the isles

There is no coconut or lemon grass here; the islands in question are Mediterranean. In a large terrine or salad bowl, lay a good-sized, gutted and scaled sea bream. Add a half-glass of olive oil, two ripe tomatoes cut into large chunks, an unsprayed lemon sliced thinly, a finely chopped bulb of fennel, a coarsely chopped onion, salt, pepper, and a pinch of saffron. Mix well and rub into the sea bream. Allow to marinate for an hour in a cool place, then pour the contents into an oven dish, pour over a half-glass of water and cook for half an hour in a low oven.

If you prefer more exotic islands, replace the saffron with lemon grass and fresh ginger, the onion with garlic cloves, the lemon with lime, and proceed in exactly the same way.

The recipe is richer and more colorful than the two before and certainly less strictly calorie-controlled—but some days are Zen days, whereas others are not.

Chicken and prawns with saffron

This dish is quick to make and a full-color people-pleaser. You will need half a chicken breast and two prawns per person. Cut the chicken breasts lengthways to make pieces the same size as the prawn tails. Remove the prawns' heads and shells. Chop two cloves of garlic. Soak a good pinch of saffron in a small cup of slightly warm water. If you have a wok, now is the time to use it, otherwise a large pan does perfectly well. Heat a little oil in the pan and cook the garlic, chicken, and prawns together on a high heat. Stir often. The cooking time should take no more than eight minutes. When they are ready, pour in the saffron and water, and a little salt. Stir the mixture for two more minutes on the stove and serve straight away decorated with cherry tomatoes and accompanied by a good, fresh salad.

Sea bream in salt crust

This is a way of cooking fish that is similar to the *en papillote* method, but even more spectacular. Choose a handsome sea bream and have your fishmonger gut and dress it, removing its fins and tail, but leaving its scales on. In a large salad bowl, mix 6^1/$_2$ lbs. (3 kg) gray sea salt with a good handful of dill seeds, lightly crushed with a mortar to bring out the aroma. Add three whole eggs and mix your salt "mortar" together well. Line the bottom of an oval gratin dish, an attractive one for serving, with this mortar to ^{1}/$_2$ inch (1 cm) thick, lay the fish on top, and fill the cavity with fresh dill, if available. Cover the sea bream with the rest of the salt mortar. Make sure the fish is coated evenly, packing the salt down. The fish should be hidden. Cook in a hot oven for half to three-quarters of an hour, depending on the weight of the sea bream. Break the salt crust in front of your guests using a sturdy knife and hammer. Remove the crust from the sides so as not to damage your fish. Serve this marvel without accompaniment. You will be surprised at how perfect it tastes.

Fish terrine

If you have leftover cooked fish, this terrine is ideal as a way of using it up. Otherwise, or as a guide to make up the weight, buy two slices of salmon and three or four fillets of whiting, and steam them for several minutes. Allow to cool and remove any skin or bones. Put several of the best pieces on one side and place the rest in a food processor with six soupspoons of ketchup, four whole eggs, ground pepper, and the juice of half a lemon. Reduce to a purée. Finely chop a bunch of chives and, in a bowl, mix these herbs into the fish purée. Cut an oval or rectangle of parchment paper to fit the bottom of a small terrine, and place it inside before pouring in half the mixture. Arrange the pieces of fish you have reserved on top of this, then cover them with the other half of the purée. Cook for three-quarters of an hour in a *bain-marie* on a gentle heat. Allow to cool completely before covering in plastic wrap and placing in the refrigerator for several hours. Turn out of the terrine and serve in slices, accompanied by a large plate of crudités and a "little sauce that makes all the difference" (see recipe page 135).

Chicken with chopsticks

The great advantage of chopsticks when trying to lose weight is that they force one to eat small mouthfuls. They are exotic, attractive, and not that difficult to manipulate. Breast of chicken cut into bite-sized pieces and marinated are perfect for serving in bowls with chopsticks. Two marinades are possible, giving results with totally different but equally delicious flavors. Allow one chicken breast per person and cut into small pieces. Peel a piece of ginger root the size of a walnut, as well as two cloves of garlic. Slice both thinly. Place the chicken, garlic, and ginger in a terrine and pour over either a half-glass of soy sauce, in which case do not add salt, or the juice of two lemons with salt and ground pepper. Mix well, cover in plastic wrap, and leave to marinate in a cool place for two hours. Heat a wok or pan. For the soy-marinated chicken, there is no need to add oil. Tip the chicken pieces with their marinade into the hot pan and cook on a brisk heat for ten or so minutes, stirring constantly. The lemon chicken will be better if you cook it with a little olive oil in the pan. Both are highly flavorsome dishes which work well accompanied by steamed vegetables. You can serve them without sauce if you want to be minimalist; otherwise a *raita* adds creamy freshness, and why not? Another possibility is to add two good handfuls of bean sprouts into the pan after the chicken has been cooking for six minutes and to cook for a further four minutes, stirring all the time. The young shoots, while they should be hot, do not really have to be cooked.

Lamb cutlets with eggplant

Order as many lamb cutlets as you have guests from your butcher. Take the largest of your gratin dishes or use the broiler pan of your oven; as the dish is destined for the table it is worth using an attractive one. Brush the bottom of the dish with olive oil and set the cutlets upright, bone in the air. Heat the oven. Wash three nice eggplants, remove their stalks but do not peel them, then cut into walnut-sized cubes. Wash three large tomatoes and cut into four.

Peel a dozen small spring onions and leave them whole. Take a dozen cloves of garlic, leaving them in their skins. You could also add strips of red pepper and cubed zucchini, but this is not necessary. Arrange all the vegetables higgledy-piggledy around the lamb pieces. Pour half an inch of water into the dish. Drizzle over olive oil. Place in the oven for one hour at 400°F (200°C) and pay attention to the final stages of cooking. Everything should be caramelized but not burnt.

Guinea fowl with cabbage

Roast a guinea fowl in a cast-iron, oval casserole dish as shown on page 44. Wash a nice green cabbage. Remove the outer leaves and stalks and cut into ½-inch (1-cm) wide strips. Blanch the cabbage for ten minutes in salted boiling water, then drain through a sieve. Peel two onions and two shallots and cut them into fine slices. When the fowl is half-cooked, remove the casserole dish from the oven and spread the vegetables around the roast. Add salt and pepper. Cover and return the dish to the oven for another half-hour. When you are about to serve, remove the roast from the oven for carving. Pour a soup-spoon of balsamic vinegar over the vegetables and mix well with the cooking juices. Serve immediately.

Rice, Pasta, Bread, Dried Pulses and Lentils, and Potatoes

As I have already said, I have tried a number of diets, and I have to confess that the most effective, initially at least—those that produced the most spectacular results, lost pounds that were alas quickly regained—were those high-protein diets where I ate only meat, fish, salad, and green vegetables. Farewell to risotto, spaghetti, and lentil salad; no more bread or potatoes. But not only did eating such a limited range of foods plunge me quickly into a permanent state of dissatisfaction, hunger, and fatigue, my mounting frustration made me, one day, launch myself at a huge plate of fries, and my fragile equilibrium crumbled along with my willpower. Separating animal protein and carbohydrates means that neither nutritional element is prohibited. Instead they are eaten alternately. The wonderful thing about this is that it allows the body to have everything it needs. Your taste buds can indulge their desires, your stomach will purr rather than rumble, and your spirit will find it all very reasonable. Rice, pasta, bread, cereals, dried beans, and pulses are irreplaceable for the quality of energy they provide. However, so that your body does not store them, you must prepare them with very little fat, eat them separately from animal proteins, and take some sort of exercise to burn them off. Here are a few recipes, from spring minestrone to the King of Samarkand's dried fruit pilaf, that for a long time I thought were forbidden. I am delighted to share them with you now.

Leeks, beans, and bread are all you need
for this delicious Baron's soup (recipe page 84).

Spring rolls

This is a highly attractive and fat-free way of presenting crudités. You will need a dozen wafer-thin round sheets of rice-flour dough, traditionally used to wrap egg rolls and spring rolls. They are readily available in Asian grocery stores and even supermarkets. Select and wash a variety of fresh, tender salad leaves and herbs, such as white or red endives, hearts of lettuce, rocket and purslane, flat-leaved parsley, mint and coriander, chives, as well as radishes, and a bulb of fennel sliced thinly. Why not add slices of apple or pear as well, or batons of cucumber, or any other tempting fresh greenery? Fill a large salad bowl with slightly warm water and spread a clean cloth on the table in front of you. Dip a round sheet of rice dough in the water for several seconds, drain it, and spread it on the cloth. In the center of the disk, lay a nice assortment of raw vegetables, herbs and salad, in a horizontal line, letting them stick out attractively on one side. Roll the sheet of rice dough around the contents to form a tight cigar. Slice the roll at one end to create a clean-cut edge, and then cut it into two equal parts. Stand the half with the protruding contents on its cut end, and lay the other one next to it, on its side. In a bowl, prepare a small dipping sauce with half a glass of water, two or three soupspoons of *nuoc-mâm*, the juice of a lime, and half a grated carrot. Each guest should have a small dish next to their plate for sauce, in which they can dip their spring rolls.

Olive *fougasse*

Olive *fougasse* has become a great classic of Provençal cookery. This recipe is unnecessary for people living in the region, as every local baker—even in the smallest villages—makes delicious *fougasses*. For those not fortunate enough to live there, or those who are tempted to have a go at making it, ask your baker to sell you an uncooked ball of dough. Incorporate thirty or so pitted olives and two soupspoons of olive oil into every 7 oz. (200 g) of dough. This means that you will have to knead the dough again until the oil is totally absorbed and the olives are evenly spread. With a rolling pin, roll out the dough to an oval shape, 1/2 inch (1 cm) thick. Place it on a floured oven tray. With a thin, sharp knife, score parallel diagonal lines across the dough or at angles in its center. Leave it to rise for an hour and a half before baking it for a good twenty minutes in a medium oven. Serve the *fougasse* slightly warm to accompany your Mediterranean vegetarian meals. Do not worry about a bread knife; it is better to tear the *fougasse* into pieces with your fingers.

Sandwiches

A truly pleasant way to eat bread! For picnics, I prefer more elaborate menus, with tablecloths and items of crockery packed in large hampers. However, simple sandwiches prepared two or three hours in advance (and all the better for it) are a perfect solution for lunch outside, especially if you are not sure exactly when you are going to eat.

In the kitchen. First prepare your palette. Lay out several types of bread on the table: wholegrain bread; leaven bread with its slightly tart aftertaste; moist, dark rye bread like pumpernickel; and delicately flavored flax, sesame, or poppy-seed bread. You will also need olive oil, tahini, and tapenade to spread on the bread, washed and rinsed green-leaf salad, sliced sweet onion and black radish, several sticks of celery, any kind of raw vegetable, some firm fruits like apples and pears, and perhaps some soft dates and shelled walnuts. If you want to be really extravagant, and it is the right season for them, finely slice a black truffle with a vegetable peeler. Once all this loveliness is spread before you, take a deep breath and let your creative inspiration do the work. Any combination is possible and (almost) all are delicious. When the sandwiches are ready, arrange them in a large dish, cover with plastic wrap, and put them in a cool place until lunchtime.

Oatmeal cream

Peel four small onions and place them in $2^{1}/_{2}$ pints ($1^{1}/_{2}$ liters) salted boiling water to cook. Meanwhile, pour a large cup of oatmeal into a salad bowl and leave to soak and swell in 16 fl. oz. ($^{1}/_{2}$-liter) soy milk. When the onions are cooked, add the oatmeal, bring back to the boil, and leave to cook for five more minutes. Liquidize in a vegetable mill, not a food processor; this is important to preserve the perfect consistency of this delicious winter soup. I can assure you that the result is worth it.

Polenta, bulgur, and quinoa
are indulgent alternatives
to rice and pasta.

Polenta and corn bread

Man was first a hunter, then he became a farmer; from then on, production of cereals and the evolution of each civilization became intimately linked. Rice cultivation originated in Asia. Alexander the Great may have brought rice from India to the Mediterranean. Certainly the Crusaders took it to France, the Moors imported it to Spain, and the Spanish shipped it to America. Wheat, of Near Eastern origin, conquered the whole of the ancient world. Pharaonic Egypt already knew all about it; not long ago, at the start of the twentieth century, Egyptologists discovered a jar full of wheat grains in a tomb, stored there three thousand years earlier. As the wheat seemed healthy, they decided to sow it. And the incredible happened, a miracle. Life had just been sleeping, and the ancient wheat grains germinated, giving birth to a "new" variety that was renamed "kamut." Today kamut wheat can be found in all organic grocery stores. Wheat has inspired a great many by-products, depending on whether the grain is coarse or fine-ground—bulgur wheat, couscous, semolina, pasta, flour, and bread.

The only cereal grain of American origin, corn, formed the basis of pre-Columbian civilizations from the dawn of time. Here are two very easy recipes, made from cornmeal. One is Italian—polenta, and the other comes from the south of the United States—corn bread.

Polenta is a simple and delicious boiled corn dish, cooked in water. Today, precooked cornmeal is easy to find, making the job easier. For each person, one cup of cornmeal needs three and a half cups of water. Sprinkle the cornmeal into salted boiling water, stir, and cook for seven minutes. Add a soupspoon of soy cream and a soupspoon of olive oil. The polenta should be of a creamy purée consistency. Serve it hot with a good, slightly thick tomato sauce, flavored with garlic and oregano.

Corn bread is also very easy to make. In a terrine, mix two cups of flour, two cups of fine cornmeal, a packet of baking powder, a pinch of salt, two glasses of soy milk, and eight soupspoons of olive oil. When the dough is of an even consistency, place it into a nonstick cake tin and cook it for twenty-five minutes in an oven preheated to 350°F (180°C). Turn out the corn bread and cut it into fine slices. Serve immediately with stewed vegetables. Cornbread is delicious hot and less appetizing cold. So do not make more than you need.

The baron's soup

This soup is not one of those precious, creamy broths, to be daintily supped from the tip of a spoon amid the tinkling of silver on porcelain. Our baron here was no doubt a hearty country fellow who, after a good day's roving with his dogs through the woods, would treat himself in the evening to this thick bread soup.

In the kitchen. Using the pan in which you will make the soup, fry two finely chopped onions in a little olive oil until golden. Clean four nice leeks, remove their roots and outer leaf, cut the green top in four and wash carefully. Slice the white parts into sections as thick as the leek is wide, and make a bundle of the green leaves tied with kitchen string. Pour 5 pints (3 liters) of salted water over the onions, add the white parts of the leek, the bundle of green leaves, and stale bread cut into cubes. Use the same volume of bread as white leek parts. Cover and cook for an hour on a low heat. In the meantime, wash and head-and-tail twenty or so large flat beans and slice them diagonally. Wash and pick over 1 lb. 2 oz. (500 g) of spinach, remove the stalks and veins from the leaves, and cut into strips. Remove the bundle of leek leaves from the soup and throw it away. It will already have given its flavor to the soup. Add the green beans and cook uncovered for a quarter of an hour to retain a good strong color. At the last minute add the spinach strips and cook for three more minutes before removing from the heat. Pour the soup into a large tureen and serve in bowls or soup dishes. Place a pepper mill and bottle of olive oil on the table so that guests can help themselves to seasoning.

Vegetable couscous

A vegetable couscous could, of course, resemble a traditional Berber couscous without the meat: carrots, turnips, zucchini and chickpeas, alongside steaming couscous semolina, sprinkled with cinnamon and served with a spicy stock, grilled almonds, and swollen sultanas. It is delicious and less calorific than one would expect. But in the Kabylia region of Algeria there is another traditional recipe for an exquisite, delightful dish. Its name eludes me, but my friends, Ounouh and Donald, have dubbed it "Frout Frout." It was Ounouh's mother who taught me how to cook it, but I have made it so often since that the recipe has evolved on its own and I'm not quite sure what the original formula was. The spirit remains and I am sure that Faroudja will forgive me.

In the kitchen. What is special about this couscous is that only a part of the vegetables are cooked in stock while the other half are stewed in olive oil in a pan. We will start with the stock. In the base section of a couscous steamer, pour $2^1/_2$ pints ($1^1/_2$ liters) of water, along with a pinch of salt, a soupspoon of ground ginger, a pinch of saffron, as well as an onion, four carrots, and four peeled and diced turnips. Add a bunch of flat-leaf parsley and one of coriander, washed and tied in bundles. As soon as the stock boils, into the top section of the couscous steamer pour 1 lb. 2 oz. (500 g) of large- or medium-grain couscous that has been pre-dampened with a little cold water: rub the grains between your hands to make sure that each one is moist. Seal the top and base of the steamer with a sheet of aluminum foil to retain the steam. Cover and wait for the steam to seep through the couscous. When it has done so, pour the couscous into a large dish, lightly salt and moisten again, breaking up any lumps. Add a chunk of squash, two zucchini, and a finely diced stick of celery to the stock and adjust the seasoning. Replace the upper part of the couscous steamer over the stock. Cover and wait for the steam to seep through the couscous. In the meantime, brown two eggplants and a red pepper, diced like the other vegetables, in a pan with a little olive oil. When they are cooked, add salt. Turn the couscous out into a large dish, drizzle over olive oil, and add the eggplants and peppers. Remove the herb bundles. Place a sieve over a salad bowl and strain the boiled vegetables. Wait for them to drain well before pouring over the couscous. Mix everything together carefully so as not to mash the vegetables. Arrange the "Frout Frout" in a dome in the middle of a large dish so that it resembles a mountain of precious stones. Serve the stock in separate bowls at the same time.

Pea and zucchini risotto

To make a good risotto, you will need round Italian "Arborio" rice: its grains will absorb the stock while remaining firm and whole.

In the kitchen. Risotto is traditionally made with chicken stock, but for this recipe, which uses peas and zucchini, we will use a vegetable stock to moisten the rice. In a large pan, pour 2½ pints (1½ liters) cold water, add salt, a well-washed leek, a zucchini, a stick of celery, an onion, half a bay leaf, and a handful of flat-leaf parsley. Cover and cook for half an hour. Meanwhile, peel and finely chop one or two onions. Wash and dice two or three young zucchinis. Shell 1 lb. 2 oz. (500 g) fresh peas. To a sauté pan, add a dash of olive oil and cook the onions over a low heat until translucent—do not allow them to go brown. Then add 10 oz. (300 g) of Arborio rice, remove from the heat, and mix until all the rice grains are coated with oil. Return to the heat and moisten with 5 tablespoons (75 ml) of dry white wine or vermouth, and stir until all the wine is absorbed. Add the zucchini and peas in the same way, continually stirring, as well as a first ladle of stock. Continue gradually adding stock; it will slowly be absorbed by the rice. The risotto should be *al dente* and smooth at the same time. When the rice is almost cooked, add a pinch of salt, a little lemon zest, and a handful of freshly grated Parmesan cheese, stirring very gently until well mixed. Add two soupspoons of olive oil and possibly a little stock to give the risotto a smoother texture. Serve immediately.

Potatoes boiled in their skins

As ever, the simpler the preparation, the more important it is to use fine quality produce to guarantee results. Choose good-quality potatoes, and perhaps potatoes with different colored skins. For example, you could use dark earth potatoes with violet flesh, "rosevals" with rosewood skin, and a paler charlotte variety. Make sure they are all the same size, so that they will take the same time to cook. They should have an attractive shape and a smooth, even surface, because we will use them whole, in their skins.

In the kitchen. Bring a large pot of slightly salted water to the boil. Carefully wash the potatoes without damaging their skins. When the water boils, add the potatoes and cook for fifteen minutes or so. Unpeeled potatoes should not cook for too long otherwise they will burst. Check they are done with the blade of a knife: it should slip in easily. When they are cooked, drain them and serve hot, with coarse salt, ground pepper, a bottle of olive oil, and a little salad lightly dresses with vinegar.

Spring minestrone

This fresh, green, tender soup from Milan is both crunchy and creamy. It should be served slightly warm and savored slowly.

In the kitchen. Finely peel and chop two cloves of garlic, a small stick of tender celery, and three small white onions. Then wash and clean 1 lb. 2 oz. (500 g) thin green asparagus. Use only the top half of each stalk and slice crossways into small ½-inch (1-cm) pieces. Place them in a salad bowl and mix together with 7 oz. (200 g) of shelled peas, 7 oz. (200 g) tender, stringless green beans, cut like the asparagus, and 10 oz. (300 g)

of small fresh fava beans, their pods and outer skin removed. In a large pan, fry the onion, garlic, and celery in very little olive oil over a low heat until golden. Then add half the vegetables. Mix with a wooden spoon and cover with 3 pints (2 liters) water. Add salt, bring to the boil, and leave to cook for half an hour. Then add the other half of the vegetables and cook for five or six minutes more. Remove from the heat, add 4 fl. oz. (125 ml) soy cream, a handful of chopped mint leaves, and several twists of pepper from a mill. Your guests do not have to hurry round for this minestrone; it is delicious served slightly warm.

Lemon spaghetti

I know that once you have tried this spaghetti, you will forgive me the very insolence of this "recipe." It is a bit of a magic trick, and the magic comes from a pint can. It has a small green cap and contains first cold-pressed olive oil and lemon oil. You will find it in Olivier and Co. stores. This might seem like a cheap ad, but the oil is honestly so divine that I use it for everything, even as a gift to friends. And when something really does the trick, you just have to tell people about it.

In the kitchen. Bring a large pan of water to the boil, sprinkle in a generous pinch of salt, and add the spaghetti almost at the same time. Follow the cooking times indicated on the side of the packet. Pour a ladle or two of the spaghetti cooking water into the serving dish. Drain the spaghetti, place in the dish, and add a generous drizzle of lemon and olive oil and a little pepper. Mix and serve immediately with just a little grated Parmesan.

Lentils with nuts

Soak 12 oz. (350 g) green lentils in cold water for 2 hours. Drain them and place them in a pan with a carefully washed and finely chopped leek, 7 oz. (200 g) shelled walnuts, and ten cloves of peeled garlic with their green inner stalk removed. Cover with $4^1/_2$ pints ($2^1/_2$ liters) cold water and bring to the boil. Lower the heat and leave to cook for an hour and a half. Season with salt and pepper when cooked. Place a sieve over a tureen and drain the lentils, then pour them into a salad bowl. On one side, you will have a delicious soup, to be served piping hot with a slice of toasted brown bread rubbed with garlic and drizzled with olive oil, while on the other you will have a lentil salad for the next day. Season the salad with a vinaigrette of olive oil, wine vinegar, a teaspoon of mustard, and a finely chopped gray shallot. Adjust the salt and pepper seasoning. At this point I just want to add a remark on cooking juices. Do not throw them away. The water from cooking vegetables makes excellent soup bases, enabling you to flavor a risotto, while meat juices are handy for an exquisite Vietnamese *phô* soup (see page 64).

The King of Samarkand's dried fruit pilaf

It is said that King Schahzaman, King of Samarkand Al-Ajam, brother of King Shahriyar and husband to Queen Scheherazade, the light of whose appearance sets the sun on fire—it is said that this great king, his wrath appeased by a thousand and one tales, regained his appetite. And that this is the exact recipe for that first dish that King Schahzaman ate. But only God really knows the truth of the tale.

In the kitchen. Break twenty or so almonds, then blanch them in boiling water for several minutes to remove their brown skins. Wipe them on absorbent paper, and toast in a low oven for ten minutes or so until golden brown. Keep an eye on them, as they must not burn. Put to one side.

In a cup, soak a good pinch of saffron in two soupspoons of rose water. Carefully wash two cups of basmati rice under running water. Add a dash of olive oil to a heavy-based pan and, over a gentle heat, fry a finely chopped onion until golden. Add two teaspoons of saffron water, then the rice, then five cups of water. Add a handful of sultanas. Increase the heat gradually, and leave to boil without stirring until small craters form on the surface. Turn off the heat. Dissolve a pinch of salt in the rest of the saffron water and pour over the rice. Drape the pan with a cloth folded in four, then cover and leave the rice to swell. It can wait for up to half an hour. At the point of serving, mix the pilaf carefully, arrange it in a mound on a hot dish. Decorate with toasted almonds and serve surrounded by mezes (see recipes pages 41 to 43).

Bulgur wheat and mushrooms

Bulgur is a particularly nutritious grain that is good to eat on cold or strenuous days, while couscous suits hot, lazy ones. Four ounces (100 g) of bulgur wheat contains 3 oz. (76 g) of carbohydrates and 10 percent water, whereas 4 oz. (100 g) of cooked couscous only contains 1 oz. (22 g) of carbohydrates, but 72.6 percent of water. Quite a surprise!

In the kitchen. In a pan on a gentle heat, cook the bulgur in two times its volume of water for half an hour. Season when cooked, mix, and keep covered until serving. The delicate nut flavor of bulgur wheat needs nothing other than a good pan of fried mushrooms as an accompaniment. Clean the mushrooms carefully, wiping them with kitchen paper. Do not wash them or, if you do so, wash them quickly; otherwise they are immediately transformed into sponges. Sauté them in a frying pan with olive oil. Add a knifepoint of chopped raw garlic and a pinch of salt when they are ready for serving.

Polpetonne

This is an old Italian family country recipe for a dish in its own right. It is eaten in the summer either slightly warm or cold with salad.

In the kitchen. In a large pan of salted water, boil a peeled onion, two leeks (white sections only), four zucchini with their skin, $1\frac{1}{2}$ pounds (800 g) of topped-and-tailed green beans, two bulbs of fennel with their outer layer removed, and $1\frac{1}{2}$ pounds (800 g) peeled and chopped potatoes. When the potatoes are cooked, add a large handful of spinach leaves or chard and leave to cook for ten more minutes. Drain, then pass through a vegetable mill, but do not blend in a food processor. In a large pan, fry two finely chopped onions in olive oil with several leaves of oregano and a sprig of rosemary. When the onions start to brown, add the purée and leave to simmer gently, while stirring, for a quarter of an hour. Remove from the heat. Now is the moment to stretch our principles slightly: add a beaten egg and a handful of grated Parmesan. (The original recipe requires four eggs and a lot of Parmesan. I have tried it without eggs and cheese, but the result is pitiful.) Cover the base of a gratin dish with breadcrumbs (simply use old dried bread whizzed in a food processor). Pour on the purée. Sprinkle on more breadcrumbs and cook in a medium oven 350°F (180°C) for forty-five minutes. Remove from the oven and leave to cool.

Fusilli with artichokes

Prepare several very young violet artichokes. Remove their stalks and the first two rows of their leaves, then cut half an inch ($1^1/_2$ cm) from their heads to the tips of their leaves. They should be young enough for the hairy part, the "choke," to be absent. Cut them into fine slices and fry in a pan with a little olive oil and three peeled cloves of garlic over a gentle heat until golden. Sprinkle over a little fresh oregano.

Season at the end of cooking. Cook the fusilli in a lot of boiling salted water until they are *al dente*. Drain the pasta and drizzle over a little olive oil. Stir and share among the plates. Crown each plate with slices of artichoke. Decorate with yellow cherry tomatoes cut in half and two or three fine curls of Parmesan shaved off using a vegetable peeler. This is all it takes—and what a treat!

Snow pea lasagna

The advantage of using flat snow peas for this recipe is that, when alternated in layers with sheets of lasagna, they make a very attractive "mille-feuille" structure.

In the kitchen. Take 2 lbs. (1 kg) snow peas, topped and tailed with their strings removed (if you choose them young and tender, there will not be any strings). Steam them in a covered sauté pan, with two soupspoons of olive oil, half a glass of water, one small lettuce cut into strips, and a chopped white onion. Ten or so minutes should be enough. During this time, prepare a tomato sauce by first peeling three cloves of garlic, removing any inner green stalks, and chopping

them into fine slices. Brown them in olive oil over a gentle heat. As soon as the garlic starts browning, add 2 lbs. (1 kg) of peeled and chopped canned tomatoes and a little salt. Leave to reduce, uncovered, for half an hour. You now need a rectangular gratin dish and a packet of lasagna sheets that require no pre-cooking. Alternate a layer of lasagna, $^1/_4$ inch (5 mm) tomatoes, a layer of snow peas packed tightly against each other, a little cooked lettuce and onions, another layer of lasagna, and so on, finishing with the tomato. From time to time, grind in a little pepper. Cook for half an hour in a hot oven and leave to cool for half an hour before serving with a little grated Parmesan or Pecorino cheese.

Vegetables

Vegetables, and especially green vegetables, have a special place in our story. Not only does their high fiber content make them indispensable, but above all they can be eaten with everything—and in the quantities you like. Red vegetables like red beet, tomatoes, and carrots have a higher sugar content, so should be consumed less frequently. Whatever the color, the best way to eat them, each and every time if possible, is raw and freshly picked, so that they retain their vitamins. For the same reason, if they need to be cooked, they should be cooked for as brief a time as possible, steaming being without doubt the best option from this point of view. However, I will demonstrate several other less rigorous, more appetizing ways of preparing them, so that you will never tire of them.

There is nothing more charming and exotic
than a nasturtium salad (recipe page 100)
shared with friends beneath a Chinese parasol.

Raw pea salad

It is important that the peas you use in this dish are very small, very fresh, and very tender. They can be difficult to find and you may have trouble in removing them from their pods, but try to overcome these difficulties because you are in for a rare treat. Once shelled, it is very likely your pea yield will be meager. This doesn't matter: just serve this "little salad" alongside others.

In the kitchen. Remove the zest from an unsprayed lemon using a vegetable peeler. On a board, cut the zest into very fine strips and blanch these in boiling water for several minutes until translucent. Drain and leave to cool. Mix the peas with rounds of finely sliced young white onion, and maybe some chopped mint leaves with a little lemon and olive oil, or just with olive oil and lemon juice, salt, and pepper.

Martin's pressed leeks

A friend of mine, Martin, is a nomad par excellence, and among the first to bring "fusion food" and *wafumi* to Paris. One day he suggested this elegant manner of presenting leeks in vinaigrette. This pressed leek dish has become staple winter fare when I invite friends over, and proves a great success every time.

In the kitchen. Select smallish leeks. Remove their roots and the base of the bulb, then their first outer skin. Wash them carefully in fresh water to remove any trace of earth. Use a good-sized rectangular terrine and trim all the leeks in such a way that they overlap the terrine by $1/2$ inch (1 cm). Bind them together with string to make two or three bundles, and cook them uncovered in salted boiling water for a good ten minutes. If the leeks are small, this should be long enough. Remove your leek bundles from the pan and keep the cooking water; it is always useful, for example, for poaching ravioli for the evening meal, or served as a thin soup with just a little pepper. Allow the leeks to drain fully. Line your terrine with plastic wrap, then lay your leeks head to tail so that they stick out of the terrine. Cover them with a second layer of plastic wrap, then lay a board on top of them and press down to squeeze out any water. Watch out for any drips. Place three cans of food on the board to weigh it down, and place the terrine in a refrigerator for about twelve hours. To serve, remove the first layer of plastic wrap, and flip over onto a dish. You should then be able to remove the second sheet carefully. You should then cut the leeks into slices and serve them using a cake slice. A vinaigrette with a lot of mustard works wonderfully with them. You can also serve them accompanied by several eggplants *à la calabraise* (see recipe page 100), an unusual combination that is rich in color and totally delicious.

Nasturtium salad

This recipe uses nasturtium buds instead of capers. These attractive orange-yellow flowers are not only edible but have a delicate peppery flavor that combines perfectly in a salad with red endive leaves split along their length and purple basil leaves. Serve accompanied by an olive-oil vinaigrette—three measures of olive oil for every one of vinegar, salt, and pepper—but leave this in a separate bowl to keep the nasturtium buds fresh.

I cannot resist sharing with you my suggestion for a winter salad, when nasturtiums are out of season and absent from your balcony or garden. Why not replace them with thin slices of black truffle? They will contrast with the endives, which are white at this time of year, and you can use hard-boiled quails' eggs to replace the basil leaves. Serve with the same vinaigrette, in the same fashion.

Alain and Max's eggplants *à la calabraise*

True bliss. Bliss as vast as the sea stretching before you, the crests of its waves dancing a light fandango. One gust of wind and there they are, stamping their feet and clapping to a flamenco rhythm. Then all is calm. Voices rise as one, joyful. Songs fill the air and faces are wreathed with smiles. This is pure happiness, full of tenderness and simplicity, just like these delicious eggplants.

In the kitchen. Choose four or five firm, plump eggplants. Their dark skin should be unblemished, as they will not be peeled. Cut them in quarters lengthways and blanch them for five or six minutes in a large pan of salted boiling water. You should drain them and leave them to cool completely. Do not worry if they still seem a little firm. Meanwhile, prepare the sauce with a half-glass of good olive oil, the same of wine vinegar, three cloves of finely chopped garlic, and a soupspoon of fresh oregano leaves. If you wish, as in Calabria, you may add a nice fresh green chili cut into rings. Pour this vinaigrette onto the eggplants. Adjust the seasoning using salt and pepper, if you have not added chili. Cover the salad bowl with plastic wrap and place in the refrigerator for one or two days. The eggplants will be much more delicious after this length of time in the marinade. They make a refreshing starter, or the perfect accompaniment for cold meat or Martin's pressed leeks (see recipe page 99).

Alain's vegetable terrine in aspic

This spectacular terrine combines all kinds of white and mainly green vegetables, but I also like to play with touches of red. I do not remember the name of the painter who said that a single touch of red on a canvas makes all the other colors vibrate.

In the kitchen. Start by heating three or four large pans of water to save time. Pre-heat the oven to 460°F (240°C) and place in it a single red pepper on a pie dish. Leave to cook until its skin is good and black. Remove from the oven and wrap in kitchen paper until it cools. Wash and clean a few shoots of green asparagus, some fine green beans and some large flat beans, five small leeks, a handful of broccoli florets, and a bulb of fennel. Shell several pods of young fava beans and peas. When the water boils, add salt to each pan, and blanch all the vegetables separately for a few minutes. The cooking water of the asparagus serves no other purpose, so can be thrown away. The vegetables should be cooked but firm—*al dente*—and have a strong color. The best way to test their readiness is to taste them: being only green vegetables, it does no harm. Remember that the broccoli cooks the quickest.

Drain the vegetables using a skimming ladle and lay them on different plates to allow them to cool. Remove the pepper from its wrapping, peel off its burnt skin and discard the seeds and white ribs from inside before cutting into fine strips. Soak nine gelatin leaves in a little cold water for ten minutes or so. Place several spoonfuls of the water in which you blanched the leek, green bean, and fennel in a pan, adjust the salt and add the juice of one lemon. Heat and add the well-drained gelatin leaves, stirring with a whisk until they are well dissolved. Allow to cool. Pour half an inch (1 cm) of this liquid into a rectangular terrine and place it in the freezer for a good ten minutes until it sets. Arrange your vegetables artistically over the aspic. Remember that aspic is transparent and that your arrangement will be visible the other side. Finish off with a layer of large flat beans to hold the construction in place. Pour over the rest of the liquid gelatin, cover with plastic wrap, and allow the terrine to set for ten minutes or so in the refrigerator. Unmold from its dish, and serve with a sauce made of two ewe's-milk yogurts beaten with salt and pepper, a little grated lemon zest, and a handful of finely chopped chives.

Gratin of chicory in beer

In northern Europe, endives are known as chicory. There is nothing simpler than this gratin. Remove the hard cone from the base of several white endives with a pointed knife, making sure the cut is not so high up the endive that the leaves fall off. Arrange the whole endives in the bottom of a heavy-based casserole dish, and pour over lager until they are submerged.

Cover and allow to cook for half an hour, then remove the cover and allow the juices to evaporate until they caramelize. Line up your endives in a gratin dish, sprinkle with a little salt and pepper. Lay on a few fine slices of *Comté* or other hard cheese and bake in a hot oven for ten or so minutes. Serve with meat or fish roasted in the oven.

Creamed zucchini

This is the easiest of all the soups to make. Wash and slice four zucchini with their skin on, then cook these along with two large peeled and sliced onions in 3 pints (2 liters) of lightly salted water for a good half-hour. Blend the veg-etables and stock in a food processor, add 2 tbs (25 ml) soy cream, several twists of the pepper mill, and a little chopped chervil. And there you go. The result is sublime, and no challenge at all to the waistline.

Roasted vegetables—my style

This is less a recipe than another way of cook-ing all sorts of vegetables together success-fully. Wash and peel the vegetables and cut into walnut-size pieces. Use olive oil to brush your broiler pan, the large dish used to catch the cooking juices from roasts. Lay your vegetables in it higgledy-piggledy, add a little salt, and driz-zle over a little olive oil. Add $1/2$ inch (1 cm) of hot water, nothing more, and cook for three-quarters of an hour in a very hot oven: 425°F (220°C). Keep an eye on them in the final stages of cooking. The vegetables should be stewed and slightly caramelized and there should be no liq-uid in the bottom of the dish. Be careful, though, because from this point on they can quickly burn. If you roast eggplants, zucchinis, tomatoes, peppers, garlic, and onions, together in this way, you will get a kind of ratatouille, less oily than the traditional recipe, which is delicious hot accompanying meat or bulgur wheat or cold as a starter. Other possible combinations are potatoes with fat slices of leek, garlic, and onion, or fleshy mushrooms, zucchini, and whole, unpeeled garlic cloves.

Spinach curry with cloves

A proper curry is nothing like a dish prepared with the generic spice mix sold in the West under that name. It is rather a spicy Indian meal made of meat, fish, or vegetables, which cleverly combines a mixture of spices. The precise combination of spices differs greatly from one recipe to the next, one region to the next, and one chef to the next. This is my spinach curry inspired by a Rajasthani recipe.

In the kitchen. Wash, sort, drain, and remove the stalks from 4^1/$_2$ lbs. (2 kg) of spinach. Roughly chop the leaves if they seem big to you. Peel and slice two good-sized onions. Heat three soupspoons of olive oil in a large sauté pan on a medium heat, with twenty or so cloves, stirring for several minutes. Then remove the cloves and sauté the onions in the oil. When the onions start to take on a golden color, add the spinach leaves and leave them to sweat, stirring constantly for ten or so minutes. Add salt and pepper and serve immediatly. Served hot, this curry makes an excellent accompaniment to fish or poultry.

Stewed vegetables

There are those days when the shopping has not been done and friends turn up to dinner unannounced. Fortunately, you have a packet of cornmeal in the cupboard to make polenta or corn bread (see recipe page 83). If you then take an assortment of vegetables from the refrigerator, a few cloves of garlic, and a can of crushed, peeled tomatoes, you have all you need to put together a delicious vegetable stew.

In the kitchen. The principle here is to follow a ratatouille recipe by mixing together all the vegetables you find. The result is surprising and always very good. Wash and peel all your vegetables except eggplants and zucchini. Cut into walnut-sized pieces. When I say "vegetables," this may include carrots, turnips, leeks, Jerusalem artichokes and potatoes, squashes and pumpkins, fennel and cabbage, as well as peppers, eggplants, and tomatoes. Finely chop a large onion. Peel several cloves of garlic and leave them whole. Using a large, heavy-based saucepan, pour in a little olive oil and fry the onion and garlic on a low heat until golden. Add the other vegetables, leaving the tomatoes until the end. If you do not have any fresh, you can always use a can of peeled and chopped tomatoes. Moisten with a glass of water. Add a bay leaf, a sprig of thyme, salt, and pepper. Mix well and raise the heat until the contents are boiling briskly. Then lower the heat once more, cover, and leave to cook gently for about three-quarters of an hour. At the end of this time, remove the cover and allow the excess juice to evaporate, stirring from time to time.

Asparagus with morel mushrooms

Morel mushrooms, along with truffles, are the only mushrooms that you absolutely do have to wash to remove the sand that nestles in their gills. This should be done quickly, beneath running water; they should definitely not be left to soak.

This dish is a starter and you will need three green asparagus stalks per person and six or seven morel mushrooms. Clean the asparagus stalks and cut them about 5 inches (13 cm) from the tip. Blanch in salted boiling water so they are still firm, then drain using a skimming ladle, and place on one side to drain on kitchen paper.

Next you should shell 1 lb. 2 oz. (500 g) small fresh fava beans and blanch for just a few minutes. Drain and remove their white outer skin. In a large pan, add a good dash of olive oil and, over a medium heat, cook the morel mushrooms, stirring and turning them frequently. When they seem to be nearly cooked, add the asparagus and fava beans, and stir gently for several minutes so that all the vegetables are coated in oil and cooking juices. Serve immediately, simply sprinkled with salt and freshly milled pepper, as a starter or as a light meal, accompanied by scrambled eggs.

Imam bayaldi

During the Ottoman era, the Turks invented more than forty ways of preparing eggplants. The masterpiece is without doubt *imam bayaldi*, which means something like "the imam swooned with pleasure." The result is so delicious that it could easily make anybody faint, including an imam.

In the kitchen. Ideally for this dish you should use small round eggplants, two per person. Wash them and, leaving the stalk attached to the fruit, split each eggplant along its length, up to the stalk. Soak them for an hour in salted water to remove their bitterness. Peel and cut three good-sized onions into thin slices. Place three large tomatoes in boiling water to remove the skin, then cut them into large cubes. Peel a dozen nice garlic cloves and leave them whole. In a pan with a little hot olive oil, brown the onion and garlic over a gentle heat. When they start to turn golden, add the tomatoes. Season and keep cooking until the juices evaporate. Wipe the eggplants to remove excess water, and stuff them generously with the onion, garlic, and tomato mixture. Arrange them in a cast-iron casserole dish. Moisten with lemon juice and half a glass of water, in which you have dissolved a teaspoon of honey. Season before replacing the cover of the casserole dish, and cook for an hour in a hot oven. Leave covered and allow to cool. Serve this delicious dish cold on a warm summer's evening.

Gratin *dauphinois* with squash and porcini

My mother's brand of cookery included fresh salads and roast meats, stews simmered for a long time, but also and above all, succulent gratins and thick soups. Her gratins and soups were unimaginable without grated cheese sprinkled over, providing one with a crisp golden crust, the other with rich gooey threads. To deprive myself forever of such a wonder, and to have to struggle to break such a delectable dependency, seemed sad and absurd to me. But, on the other hand, daily and abundant use of grated Gruyère cheese was without doubt going to be prejudicial to the success of my enterprise. There are three qualities to this ingredient: its taste, smell, and its many textures. Its taste and aroma depend on the quality of the cheese. Everybody knows that industrial Emmenthaler sold as a vacuum-packed brick has little in common with a slice of farm-churned Gruyère or *Comté* from a good producer, who has matured the cheese with all the necessary care and attention. A good cheese is one that can be used in cookery as a herb or a spice, that is to say, in small quantities, and in this way is no threat to any weight-loss plan. However, achieving a good melted cheese texture implies the use of larger quantities of cheese. So it should not be eaten with carbohydrates in the same meal, and fatty accompaniments should be limited.

Gratin dauphinois, one of my mother's triumphs and a great childhood treat, is today reserved for times of sin and celebration, but I have perfected a squash-based version that enables me, from time to time, to indulge in all the joys of a melted surface crust and oozing grated cheese deep within the gratin.

In the kitchen. Remove the skin from a 2 lb. (1 kg) slice of butternut squash, available from the month of September to the end of winter. Clean 2 lbs. (1 kg) of healthy, firm porcini mushrooms, using a knifepoint to remove all traces of earth. Above all, do not wash them, as they will fill with water. Cut the squash and mushrooms into 1/2-inch (1-cm) slices no finer as we are not making fries here. Grate 5 oz. (150 g) of a good farm-made *Comté* cheese, or similar hard cheese. Rub a gratin dish well with a clove of garlic until the clove is used up. Begin by putting in a layer of squash slices, then a layer of mushroom slices, and sprinkle with a little grated cheese, ground pepper, and the slightest pinch of salt. Alternate squash and mushroom layers until the ingredients run out. Sprinkle over the remains of the cheese and pour over the contents of a pint (1/2 liter) of soy cream, the non-dairy vegetable-based cream I have already told you about. Cook for an hour and a half in a gentle oven. Midway through cooking, press the vegetables down lightly using a potato masher, without crushing them, to bring the juice to the surface.

Serve hot with a salad of frisé lettuce hearts, seasoned with a dash of vinegar, olive oil, and garlic, and a large slice of crusty bread.

BREAKFASTS AND DESSERTS

A tablecloth, attractive crockery, a bowl of fruit, a ray of sunshine glancing on the table, perhaps a real fire or a candle if it is too early in the morning—or, if it is warm, the window thrown open, with the morning streaming in. Staging. That's all it involves: a small amount of staging, which takes three minutes to install, to create that special ambience. And then you will need further time, twenty minutes at the most, in order to enjoy breakfast. Breakfast should be a real meal, a hot one in winter, which prepares the body for the day, giving it energy. In summer, your breakfast will be more refreshing, but still contain all you need to face the day's tasks. Adapt your menus to the season and circumstances. If your program includes shopping, or rambling in the mountains, you will need more energy than if you were working in an office, so such a day should be a carbohydrate day. For real indulgence, you could finish up a dessert from the night before. If excesses occur at breakfast time they will be eliminated sooner than if they take place later in the day. So make the most of the moment of calm and pleasure before setting into action. Have a very nice day!

As for desserts, I have chosen the mainly low-fat (though some are not at all) and low-sugar (all are more or less) recipes from my repertoire. None are really compatible with serious weight loss. Weight cannot be lost eating butter, sugar, and chocolate. It is important, here more than ever, to learn to measure out your portions, to be your own alchemist, and carefully compose your menus. If you want to serve a dessert that contains a fair amount of sugar, have it at the end of a very low-fat meal—and tuck in.

After a slice of chocolate cake (recipe page 131) and a cup of tea for breakfast, make sure that dinner is lighter than usual.

Soft-boiled eggs and chicken fingers

There is nothing easier to prepare. There is no need to tell you at this point that you should only buy the freshest eggs, from farmyard chicken, running free with the rooster, fed on wheat or corn. Without doubt that is the hardest part of the recipe! Remove the eggs from the refrigerator the night before so that they are not cold when you place them in boiling water, as the sudden change of temperature will often break the shell. Boil a small pan of water, place your eggs in it gently, using a soupspoon, and leave them to cook for three minutes exactly. You then need to eat them quickly or slice open the top; otherwise they will continue to cook and you will not be able to dunk your chicken fingers.

You will already have realized that fingers of crusty bread smeared in creamy rich butter are not permitted. Banish them to that department of your memory that contains lost pleasures from the garden of Eden, Eldorado, or the undersea world of Atlantis. (I make sure I catch up with such memories every time I go to Paris, when I breakfast at the Café de Flore, where the soft-boiled eggs are sublime and the fingers of bread and butter are divinely non-dietary—but don't tell anyone!) However, if, the evening before, while preparing the dinner, you steam or cook *en papillote*—one or two chicken breasts, in the morning you will be able to cut perfect fingers to dunk into the egg yolk. It is very easy. Wrap the chicken breasts in a piece of aluminum foil and lay the parcel in the basket of the steamer or in a sieve above a pan of boiling water. A quarter of an hour is enough. Leave them to rest in their parcels until the following morning so that the chicken breast does not dry out.

To recap: For a perfect breakfast you will need soft-boiled eggs in attractive egg cups, sea salt and pepper, chicken breast fingers, a small horn or pearl spoon, as silver gives egg yolk a nasty flavor, a cup of coffee or Ceylon tea, and a piece of fruit.

Turkish breakfast

Here is an ideal summer breakfast: one where you can open the window, and let in the sun and gentle fresh morning, and then dream you are on the banks of the Bosphorus.

Serve tea in glasses and arrange, in as many dishes, thickly sliced ewe's cheese in salt water, such as Greek feta; thinly sliced ewe's cheese with a crust, such as *tomme* from the Pyrenees; several small goat's cheeses; some hard or soft-boiled eggs removed from their shells; a firm cucumber, peeled and cut into sticks, and some tomato quarters, more or less ripe according to taste. This breakfast needs no bread, but it does need olives, all kinds—black, green, and purple.

Scrambled eggs and mushrooms

Scrambled eggs are a more difficult exercise. The secret is in the thickness of the pan you use, and a non-stick base. I love making this recipe with freshly gathered field mushrooms. The delicateness of their texture is ideal for this morning moment, and their taste is like nothing else. Start by beating the eggs in a bowl. You will need two per person. Add a soupspoon of olive oil, and one of water, salt, and pepper, and beat again, although not too much—we are not making zabaglione. Place a pan on a low heat with another soupspoon of olive oil. When the oil is hot, add two handfuls of mushrooms with the strands of grass removed. Do not wash them, though: they will soak up water like a sponge. Cook them until they melt, stirring with a wooden spoon. This will take no time at all as they are only small. Add the beaten eggs and keep stirring as they start to harden at the edges of the pan. The most difficult part is knowing when to stop. Scrambled eggs should be creamy at the point you place them on the plate. As they continue cooking in the hot pan, and even when you have turned off the heat, it is absolutely necessary to anticipate this and remove them from the heat when they are not quite cooked. I promise that, with a small amount of practice, you will quickly get the knack.

Mauritian omelet

Here is a breakfast to help you dream of white sands, huge shells, a turquoise lagoon, and white and pink bougainvilleas dancing lightly in the air. I brought this bright, invigorating recipe back from Mauritius where, each morning, as part of a buffet featuring masses of fruit and all the brioches on earth, a very young chef, wearing a hat taller than himself, would brilliantly knock up one of these omelets in a minute.

In the kitchen. You need to prepare small, individual omelets. If there are several of you, make the omelets one after the other. They are very quick to prepare anyway. In a bowl, break two fresh free-range eggs. Add a soupspoon of chopped tomato, a soupspoon of raw, diced scallion, and a soupspoon of grated Gruyère. Split a green chili pepper in two and remove its seeds, as the seeds are the hottest part. Cut the pepper into very fine strips and add a teaspoon of these to the bowl. Add a pinch of salt. You can now start beating the eggs with their garnish. Heat a small, non-stick pan and, only when it is hot, pour in the beaten eggs. Pull away the edges of the omelet from the side of the pan as they cook, drawing them toward the center of the pan, using a wooden spoon. The omelet should be stirred constantly so as not to brown. Two or three minutes on the heat should suffice. Serve immediately, folded in two, accompanied by a piece of fruit (a good slice of fresh pineapple, for example) and a large cup of green tea.

Eggs and bacon

This is an English breakfast dish par excellence. You will need two non-stick pans, because we are going to cook using only the fat of the bacon. Even this way, the dish is not ideal for losing weight, I know. But if you follow my advice and you always vary your breakfast formula, you can indulge yourself from time to time with this English treat without any worries.

Warm your oven to 300°F (150°C). Heat two sauté pans and, as soon as they are hot, lay in two fine slices of not-too-fatty bacon to brown. When they are fried golden on one side, turn them over to fry until golden on the other. Remove from the pan and keep warm in the oven, where they will continue to grill gently. In the first pan, lay several whole mushrooms without stalks and one or two tomatoes cut in half, turning them in the bacon fat. Break the eggs into the other pan and lower the heat. They will cook gently and remain moist. When everything is ready, place two eggs, a half-tomato, several mushrooms, and two slices of crunchy bacon on each plate.

The *"coucourde fougasse"*—stuffed squash bread

This can be served as a dessert for autumn or a good breakfast indulgence.

Start by preparing the dough, as it has to rise. In a terrine, mix $1/2$ oz. (20 g) of fresh bread yeast in a half-glass of slightly warm water. Add a pinch of salt, 10 oz. (300 g) brown flour and half a glass of olive oil. Mix, then knead vigorously until the dough is smooth, supple, and does not stick to the hands. Make a ball, place it in a salad bowl, cover with a clean cloth, and leave to rise for an hour and a half at room temperature. During this time, prepare the stewed squash. In a pan on a low heat, cook a slice of peeled and diced butternut squash with a half-glass of water and a handful of raisins. After half an hour, add a soupspoon of liquid honey.

Continue cooking, stirring all the time, until it has the consistency of jam. Remove from the heat and leave to cool.

Knead the dough once again, then divide it into two equal parts. With a rolling pin, roll out two same-size $1/2$-inch-thick ovals. Lay one of them on a floured oven tray. Spread the squash stuffing in the middle of the dough to within $1/2$ inch (1 cm) of the edges. Cut three or four diagonal lines through the thickness of the second oval and place it on the first to cover the stuffing. Seal the edges and leave the *fougasse* to rest and rise once more for an about hour and a half. Cook for thirty-five minutes in a medium oven. The *fougasse* should be golden and not burnt. Leave to cool before serving.

Yogurt with honey

Another summer breakfast, from the Aegean Sea, made up of a good slice of ripe, succulent watermelon and ewe's-milk Greek yogurt, coated with just the right amount of runny amber Greek honey. If you cannot find any watermelon, prepare a plate of fruit pieces. Peel the pears and peaches into quarters and leave the skin on the apple slices.

Mrs. Angus' porridge

One of my favorite utensils is quite simply a wooden stick, rounded off like a thin pestle at one end, and decorated at the other end with a sculpted wooden thistle, the emblem of Scotland. This utensil, called a *spurtle*, is used to stir porridge while it is cooking, and was given me, a long time ago, by Mrs. Angus, a gentle, generous woman who made the best porridge in Aberdeenshire. Don't worry if you do not have a similar treasure: you will find a good wooden spoon works just as well.

Like polenta, spelt soup, and buckwheat groats, porridge is one of those concoctions of boiled cereals that can sometimes resemble wallpaper paste, but can also be transformed into a truly delicious meal. To achieve this miracle first time, be sure to follow this advice to the letter. I picked up this recipe more than thirty years ago, while on a trip to Scotland to learn English, and carefully copied it into my cookery scrapbook.

The success of porridge depends on the quality of your oatmeal. The oatmeal that the Scots use has clearly been ground much finer than that generally available. You can easily remedy this problem by giving coarser oats a quick whiz in the food processor, but not for too long: flour is not ideal for this recipe. Porridge should retain a grainy yet creamy texture.

In the kitchen. You will need a saucepan and 16 fl. oz. ($^1/_2$ liter) water for four servings, to which you should add a pinch of salt. Bring the salted water to a gentle boil and sprinkle in two large handfuls of oatmeal, stirring all the while. Lower the heat and leave to cook gently for ten or so minutes, even longer if you have the time. Stir often so that the porridge does not stick. Remove from the heat and stir in a teaspoon of virgin sesame oil. Pour this creamy porridge into four bowls and serve immediately with fresh soy milk in a jug and brown, superfine sugar.

Nut butter bread slices

As you may have grasped by now, bread and butter do not get on well together. However, as giving up crusty slices of bread smeared with butter for ever is an impossibility, make sure you select a really fresh loaf of bread from a genuine baker: it can be wholegrain or brown, spelt, kamut, or granary—whatever you like. And replace dairy butter with nut butter, made from peanuts, hazelnuts, almonds or sesame seeds. In this way the meal will be energy-rich and totally vegetable-based, with no conflicting foodstuffs. Nut pastes are rich in lipids and very nourishing. Spread just a fine layer on the bread and sweeten it with a final, thin coating of honey. Tuck in and treat yourself, before walking the dog for longer that morning.

Granola

In California, it seems that a great part of the population is concerned about their figure. People run or cycle all over the place, water bottle at the ready. Nobody smokes, and food substitutes are on sale everywhere. There are vast, wonderful organic food stores that are infinitely more appetizing than most of our sad health shops in Europe. However, when it comes to fruit, vegetable, and poultry selections, despite the abundance, variety, and freshness on the shelves in Californian stores, I still prefer the markets of Provence. But the range of cereal grains in these organic stores is exceptional, featuring every variety of rice and wheat from around the world, including Egyptian kamut, bulgur wheat from Anatolia, spelt from Sault, quinoa from the Andes, and rolled couscous semolina of every grade. Also available are yellow, white, and blue cornmeal, muesli blends, and twenty varieties of granola. Granola is a delicious combination of oatmeal and dried fruits and nuts, flavored with cinnamon and grilled in the oven with a little honey to make it crunchy. I first came across it in California. It is served at breakfast with cold milk and fresh fruits. Here is my favorite recipe.

Start by soaking $3^1/_2$ oz. (100 g) of dried apricots cut into small pieces with $3^1/_2$ oz. (100 g) raisins in $^1/_2$ pint ($^1/_4$ liter) of hot water. Then heat the oven to 250°F (120°C). In a large bowl, mix $12^1/_2$ oz. (350 g) of oatmeal with 2 oz. (50 g) of raw sunflower seeds, 2 oz. (50 g) flaked almonds, two soupspoons of liquid honey, and a teaspoon of ground cinnamon. Add the soaked dried fruits and their water and stir carefully. Spread this mixture on an oven tray, place in the oven, and roast the granola for an hour, stirring from time to time. Allow to cool completely before storing it in a closed container in which it will keep a week. Serve for breakfast or dessert in a bowl, covered in soy milk.

Muesli

Organic grocers, and even large supermarkets, today sell a vast range of combinations of cereals and dried fruits under this name. There are oatmeal muesli mixtures with five cereal grains and red fruit, with amaranth, quinoa, or coconut. The traditional Swiss recipe is more frugal and simple, and I find it delicious as it is. Here it is: start by washing and wiping a nice firm apple, one that is not too ripe. Cut it into four and remove the core from each quarter, but leave the skin it is full of vitamins and will add a splash of color to the muesli. Coarsely grate the apple. In a salad bowl mix the grated apple with two cups of oatmeal, a handful of raisins, a few less hazelnuts and enough soy milk to create a thick cream. And that is all there is to it!

Strawberry and raspberry cake

Wash 9 oz. (250 g) of strawberries and remove their stalks. Place them in a terrine with a soupspoon of caster sugar and the juice of an orange. In another terrine, crush 9 oz. (250 g) of raspberries with a fork and mix them together with two pots of yogurt. Line the bottom of a cake tin with a sheet of parchment paper. Arrange a layer of ladyfinger biscuits, neatly packed together, rounded side downwards on the paper. Spread over a layer of raspberry yogurt, then a layer of strawberries. Add another layer of biscuits, and so on, finishing with the biscuits, ideally to a level just higher than the cake tin. Lay on another sheet of paper, then place a board on top and weigh it down with three cans. This will remove the air pockets between the biscuits, but might also force some of the sponge cream out. This is not a problem. Just wipe any excess off and place for half an hour in the freezer, then three hours in the refrigerator. Turn out and decorate the top of the cake with several attractive strawberries.

Pears in wine

Peel ten or so pears, leaving the stalk on. You will need flavorsome, firm but not too hard, cooking pears. In a pan, line the pears up, one against the other, in rows like soldiers. Cover them with 16 fl. oz. (¹/₂ liter) of good red wine and the same quantity of Muscat. Add the zest from two unsprayed oranges, a stick of Ceylon cinnamon and two cloves, as well as two soupspoons of honey. Bring to the boil, then lower the heat and poach the pears slowly for twenty minutes. Remove from the heat and allow to cool in the wine before serving.

Compote of fruits

I make sure that I always have fresh fruit at home. Often, even though I have already bought peaches and pears, I cannot resist the temptation of apricots. And then, on returning from market and emptying my basket, I find I have clearly bought ten times too much. This is the moment to make stewed fruit. Using sweet, juicy summer produce, this is an easy recipe. Peel white and yellow peaches and cut them into segments. Peel the pears, cut them into four to remove the core, then cut again into smaller pieces. Mix the fruits in a pan and cook on a medium heat, stirring frequently with a wooden spoon so that the caramel forming around the edges of the pan dissolves gradually and does not burn. The fruit should stew for about quarter of an hour. For autumn fruits, which have less juice and sugar, proceed in the following manner: Peel and cut four pears, four apples, and a quince into pieces. What varieties of apples and pears you use is not important. You may use different ones of each. Mix the slices of fruit in the pan with a glass of water and a handful of raisins, for the sweetness they bring. If you cannot find quinces,

which help to add flavor, you may instead add, according to tastes, a split vanilla bean pod, a stick of Ceylon or Chinese cinnamon, the zest of an unsprayed lemon, two or three cloves, or a little pepper. Cool these fruits just as you did the summer ones, then pour into an attractive bowl and serve slightly warm or cold, with low-fat *fromage blanc*. This is good as a dessert or for breakfast.

Fezan's red fruit jelly

Gentle Fezan was born on the shores of the Bosphorus, in the shelter of one of those elegant wooden *yallis*. She speaks delightfully of her country's delicate embroidery, the aromas of its rosewater and coffee, and the smooth sweetness of its jams and stewed fruits, the pride of Turkish cookery. She gave me this recipe for a translucent, slightly tart jelly that shivers in its serving dish. Here it is:

Soak eight gelatin leaves in a bowl of cold water for about ten minutes to soften them. Dry them between your hands, heat $3\frac{1}{2}$ fl. oz. (100 ml) of water, then slowly melt the gelatin. Add three soupspoons of red fruit cordial. It is the only sugar to go into this recipe, and it will give the jelly a lovely rich color. Add the juice of half a lemon, a glass of Muscat wine, or the juice of a freshly squeezed orange, and allow the mixture to cool completely. Then pour two fingers of this liquid into the bottom of a mold and place in the refrigerator until the jelly sets. Ten minutes should be enough. Keep the rest of the jelly at room temperature, as it should remain liquid until ready for use. During this time, prepare your fruit. You will need twenty or so strawberries, two handfuls of raspberries, another of blackberries, several cranberries, and just a few redcurrants—the dessert is not excessively sweet, and too many redcurrants could make it too tart. Wash the strawberries and redcurrants and remove their stalks. Clean the other fruits. When the jelly base has set, arrange a layer of fruit over it, bearing in mind that jelly is transparent and your fruit arrangement will be visible through the base when the mold is turned upside down for serving. Cover the first layer of fruit with liquid jelly, and replace the mold in the refrigerator. Continue in this manner with successive layers until all the jelly has been used and the last fruits just break the surface. Cover the mold with plastic wrap and chill until the next day. Turn out the fruit red jelly just before serving. This dessert is spectacular, fresh and only slightly sweet. It is also delicious made with peaches, pears, and mangoes, or clementine quarters and segments of orange flesh and grapefruit cut from the pith. You may use honey in place of the red fruit cordial, and a verbena or mint tea in place of the water.

Chocolate cake

The devil's own gateau, that irresistible temptation, is not as demonic as all that. It was not so long ago that I would make the same recipe adding 6 oz. (150 g) of sugar. One day I attempted the recipe adding no extra sugar other than that already in the chocolate itself, and I liked the result. On the day you prepare this, make a light meal, like fish and green vegetables, and declare war on your feeling of guilt rather than your sense of indulgence. One last piece of advice: take a good slice of this cake—it is worth it—but no second helpings!

In the kitchen. Make this cake the night before you want to eat it. It tastes much better the next day, or even the day after that. Break 10 oz. (300 g) chocolate (with 70 percent cocoa content) into small pieces and melt in a *bain-marie*, stirring constantly as soon as it starts to melt. Do not heat it too much or the flavor will be altered. When the chocolate has melted, remove from the heat and stir in 3 oz. (75 g) of butter then, one by one, three whole eggs, stirring constantly. Finally, stir in 3 oz. (80 g) of sieved flour. Pour this mixture into a flexible mold, as chocolate cake is difficult to turn out; using this marvel of modern technology will make it easier. Cook for fifty minutes in a *bain-marie* in a medium oven at 350 °F (180 °C). Turn the cake out directly onto its serving dish as it does not take kindly to handling. Leave to cool completely before covering in plastic wrap and keeping cool (though not in the refrigerator) for at least twenty-four hours.

Apple and pear *clafoutis*

This is another recipe from childhood that brings back so many happy memories that I could not scrub it from my repertoire. While my mother's recipe did not include fat, it combined milk, eggs, and flour, and it seemed impossible to replace any of these ingredients. I thus decided to alter the quantities and, after several experiments, I arrived at an excellent result. This is the recipe.

In the kitchen. As it is the batter that poses the problems, we are going to make less of it and increase the quantity of fruit. Peel and cut into pieces five pippin apples and five flavorsome pears that are firm but not too hard. In a terrine, mix five level soupspoons of flour with two level soupspoons of crystallized fructose, which is now readily available in organic stores. Add a small pinch of salt before pouring in 16 fl. oz. ($^1/_2$ liter) of zero percent fat skimmed milk and stirring with a whisk. Keep beating and add five whole eggs, one by one. Pour the fruits into this preparation. Mix well to coat each piece of fruit and arrange in a gratin dish. Cook for three-quarters of an hour in an oven at 350°F (180°C). The *clafoutis* is delicious slightly warm and marvelous cold. Sometimes, on winter evenings, we make this the only dish of the meal.

SEVERAL RECIPES FOR THE MORNING AFTER

Let's not talk about what you got up to last night. I hope that it was delicious and that you kicked loose and had a ball. Today, it is time to return to the path of reason, correct your excesses, pacify your body, detoxify and purify it, and prevent it from believing that it needs to build an extra cushion. However, rather than punishment, quite the opposite: we are going to cure with kindness. In the morning, go for muesli with soy milk so as not to die of starvation, or fruit, or a simple yogurt. Follow your instincts, but do eat breakfast, even a very light one. For lunch, go for vegetables, and a little rice or an egg. Then for dinner have a plate of *"aïgo boulido"* or a bowl of "nothing-to-it" soup (see recipes pages 136 and 36). In the morning, prepare a large pot of herbal tea. Drink it hot for breakfast and cold throughout the day. Indulge yourself with gentle therapy like this and enjoy its simplicity. Take time out to look after yourself. It is the moment to go running or swimming, then to relax in a good bath, have a long shower, or a massage. It is the perfect day to go to the *hammam*. True happiness will be reached the day after tomorrow when you will feel light and at peace for having washed out the toxins that still troubled you the night before. The following recipes will enable you, according to the weather and season, to match your menu to your mood, whether you are feeling delicate, frugal, ethereal, or deliciously masochistic, ascetic, unadventurous, rustic, or sophisticated. You will even have the right to indulge.

Fine slices of Parma ham and figs crammed with sunshine (recipe page 139) are well matched by the mellow, sweet freshness of verbena and lemon zest iced tea (recipe page 140).

Three florets and a "little sauce that makes all the difference"

I have been meaning to tell you for a long time to buy a Chinese steamer, that is to say a large pan mounted with three perforated, perfectly fitting baskets with a cover. You can use it to cook nearly all your vegetables, fish, *papillotes* and raviolis. You can even flavor the steam with herbs and spices according to what you fancy. This ideal method of cooking preserves not only vitamins but also the true taste of things.

In the kitchen. Take, for example, a white cauliflower, a Romanesco cauliflower, and two heads of broccoli. Separate the florets of your vegetables and place the white cauliflower in one of the steamer baskets, the Romanesco cauliflower in another, and the broccoli in the third. Heat the water in the pan. When it is boiling well, lay on the first two baskets and cover to keep in the steam. After seven minutes, add the broccoli basket. Cover again for three minutes. The three vegetables must be cooked absolutely *al dente*. Arrange in a pyramid, alternating them, playing on the three colors. Serve them slightly warm or completely cooled. For the sauce, take a handful of flat parsley, several mint leaves, six soupspoons of olive oil, the juice of a lemon, and a pinch of salt, and place in a food processor bowl. Blend the sauce and serve in a bowl alongside the steamed vegetables.

Braised lettuce with anchovies

This exquisite braised lettuce was my grandmother Athalie's traditional remedy, used when someone in the family was suffering from any of those nonspecific upsets that meant you were feeling out of sorts. It is a little bitter, slightly sour, and a touch spicy. It would almost be medicine if it were not such good cuisine. With every mouthful, you can feel it doing you good.

In the kitchen. You need three fresh, crisp lettuces per person; they need not necessarily be firm and hearty. Cut a slice from the stem but leave them whole, wash them carefully, and drain them quickly; you need to have a small amount of the water clinging to their leaves for cooking.

Peel and slice four or five cloves of garlic after removing the inner green stalk. In the base of a big casserole dish, add a dash of olive oil, and fry the garlic slices golden. As soon as they start to color slightly, arrange your lettuces in the dish, packed against each other. Cover and leave to cook for ten minutes. During this time, clean six salted anchovies in fresh water. Remove their fins and bones and place the fillets to one side. Turn the lettuces, so that they brown on their other side for another ten minutes. Arrange the braised lettuce in a hot serving dish and, over the heat, fry the anchovy fillets in the lettuce cooking juices so that they melt. Pour this anchovy mixture over the lettuces and serve immediately.

A bowl of rice

It is good to get back to the bare essentials, though even the Buddhist priest who gives up his wordly possessions may retain five objects: a robe, a book of prayers, a parasol, a fan, and a bowl for rice.

In the kitchen. Soak a cup of brown rice in three times its volume of water for an hour.

Then cook it in its soaking water for thirty-five minutes. Turn off the heat, cover, and leave the rice to swell for ten more minutes. Drain it and serve it in a bowl, with chopsticks, accompanied by *gomasio*, a mixture of salt and grilled, crushed sesame seeds, which will season your rice and lend a delicate flavor that will go well with the gentle, nutty flavor of brown rice.

The "*aïgo boulido*"

"Boiled water": the easiest soup in the world to make. In Provençal dialect people say, *"L'aïgo boulido sauvo la vido"* ("Boiled water saves lives"), and indeed this soup is miraculous the day after a blow-out meal or during a nasty bout of the flu. However, they also add, not unphilosophically and not without humor, *"Au bout d'un tems, tuo li gènt"* ("After a while, it kills people"), which means that man cannot live on boiled water alone! Come what may, it is delicious and absolutely harmless.

In the kitchen. You will need three or four cloves of garlic per person. Leave them in their skins and crush them slightly on the table with the palm of the hand. Boil them for ten minutes or so in salted water. Then extinguish the heat, add a little thyme, a bay leaf, and a lot of sage. Cover and leave to infuse. You should then strain the stock and reheat it slightly without boiling it, then serve it in a soup tureen with slices of grilled bread, drizzled with a little olive oil in the plates.

Vegetable stock and its vegetables

Here is another recipe for "boiled water" that is fortifying and constitutes a whole meal—a plate of vegetables, a bowl of hot stock, a drizzle of olive oil, and a dash of lemon juice. Wash and peel three leeks, three zucchinis, an onion, and a stick of celery. The flavors and aromas of these four vegetables will combine marvelously.

Leave them whole and place them in $2^1/_2$ pints ($1^1/_2$ liters) of salted boiling water. When the water boils again, lower the heat and leave to cook for twenty minutes or so. Remove the vegetables using a skimming ladle, and serve them immediately accompanied by a bowl of stock sprinkled with a pinch of finely chopped chives.

Purslane salad with soft-boiled eggs

Today fresh purslane is increasingly available, no doubt due to the media success of the Cretan diet, in which purslane is an emblematic leaf, a guarantor of long life. Make the most of this abundance. It is an excellent green leaf, both tender and fleshy. Wash and drain several handfuls of purslane leaves. Mix in several leaves of flat-leaf parsley, several fine slices of cucumber, and several thinly sliced rounds of sweet onion.

Then, soft boil an egg for about five minutes, I would say, depending on the size of the egg. The white should be totally cooked, the yolk creamy, between runny and hard and not completely solid. Beware soft-boiled eggs are very difficult to shell. Place the egg at the center of the salad, drizzle over olive oil and add several drops of balsamic vinegar (without touching the egg), and a pinch of coarse sea salt.

Figs and Parma ham

What a happy marriage! The flavor of Parma ham, enhanced by being finely sliced, and the sweetness of the figs, swollen with sunshine, blend together wonderfully. Soak the ripe figs in a salad bowl with water and ice cubes for about ten minutes. Wipe them carefully. Cut them in four starting from the tail without going right to the end of the fruit. On each plate, lay three figs intermingled with a thin slice of Parma ham. Serve immediately or cover in plastic wrap and keep cool until the last moment. Raw ham hates to be warmed up.

Spinach and poached eggs

This recipe takes me back to the olden days, when I spent most nights strutting my stuff to pop and psychedelia and drinking far too many vodka-oranges. It was summer and the *meltémi* wind made the waves of the Aegean Sea curl, chasing away the clouds in the sky without managing to disperse the mist that clouded our minds each morning. The lunch menu was always the same—spinach and poached eggs. Contrary to received ideas, spinach does not contain, or ontains very little, iron. However, it is rich in vitamin C, which revitalizes and chases away sluggishness, so this is perfect for the morning after.

In the kitchen. Use fresh, tender spinach leaves with a good, deep-green color. Wash them prior to preparation, quickly but carefully, to remove all traces of sand and earth. Shake gently; the remaining water in the leaves will be enough for cooking them. This will take three minutes on a brisk heat in a covered pan. Season at the end of cooking. Poaching the eggs is a slightly more delicate operation. Heat two inches of water, with a splash of added vinegar, in a wide, shallow pan, until it simmers. Use very fresh eggs so that, when you break them, their yolks stay intact. (If you are not completely sure of the absolute freshness of your eggs, make scrambled eggs instead.) Break an egg in a cup, then let it slip gently into the hot water. This should not change its form too much. Repeat the operation for each egg. Leave to simmer for four minutes. Keep the heat very low: the water should not boil. Remove the eggs using a skimming ladle and lay them on the spinach. Serve them as they are with coarse sea salt and maybe a little pepper. The soft eggs make a sublime sauce for the spinach.

"Prés d'Eugénie" slimming tea, herbal teas, and iced tea

If you have never vacationed at the "Prés d'Eugénie" in Eugénie-les-Bains, in the southwest of France; if you have never bathed in the waters there, or sat in its dining room to delight in its dishes and nectars, you will not be aware of the marvelous brew my friend Christine Guérard has concocted—her slimming infusion. It is a mix of heather, corn silk, horsetail, bearberry, and cherry stalks. The taste of this would probably, like most herbal teas, be a bit sharp, and force you to say to yourself as consolation: "It's just as well it's doing me good!" However, you add half a lemon, half an orange, and a small bunch of fresh mint to counteract the sharpness. It is served in a large glass with ice. Add one more slice of fruit and the potion turns into a cocktail, while the remedy becomes an indulgence. This is perhaps one of the most important secrets of this book.

Herbal teas, to take effect, should be drunk often, several times a day and over a period of about a month. A number of medicinal properties, some incontestable, are attributed to herbs. This time-honored knowledge is passed on by word of mouth from generation to generation. Scientists, generally reticent, nevertheless often confirm some of these benefits. The best way to profit from the qualities of these plants is to do so in infusions and decoctions. Infusing a herbal tea consists simply of placing leaves into very hot but not boiling water, and leaving them to brew. A decoction means boiling the leaves in water for several minutes then leaving to infuse. Herbal medicine is a vast and complex subject and it is a good idea to be advised by an expert. There are no problems, however, when it comes to using the most common herbs such as thyme, rosemary, verbena and lime, savory and mint. Unlike coffee and tea, herbal teas contain no tannin or caffeine. I regularly prepare a delicious tea-less "iced tea" that I serve as an appetizer in the summer.

In the kitchen. In a teapot, prepare an infusion of fresh verbena. Fill a large clear jug of ice with an unsprayed lemon cut in half and slightly squeezed, along with a bunch of fresh mint slightly crumpled between your hands. All that remains for you to do is to pour the hot brew over the ice cubes and wait for them to melt. Sometimes I replace the verbena with hibiscus flowers, which gives the tea a delightful pink color. Do not be surprised by the absence of sugar in this recipe; it is sufficiently fresh and flavorsome to do without.

Table of Recipes

Recipe Index

Thanks to Nick and Sugar for finally agreeing to pose for us with their bone.
Thanks to Frankie and Tench, my marvelous American friends,
their children, and grandchildren, for their hospitality.
Thanks to Irène, Kathryn, Sandra, Faroudja, Lan, Fezan, and to
Alain and Max, Régis, Martin, Olivier, Piero, Patrick, Alain, Dan,
Gérard, and Tadeusz for their delicious recipes.
Thanks to Yves, Stéphane, Christophe, my fitness coach, and all my friends at the
Sportislois club for their friendly smiles, outstretched hands, and valuable advice.
Thanks to Gilles Martin-Raget for his talent and his unfailing complicity.
Thanks finally to Gisou Bavoillot, my publisher and friend.

Translated from the French by Jonathan Sly
Copyediting: Penny Isaac
Typesetting: Thomas Gravemaker
Proofreading: Susan Kennedy
Color separation by Penez Édition

Originally published as *Et Mincir de Plaisir: Cuisine légère et art de vivre* © Flammarion 2003
English-language edition © Flammarion 2003

03 04 05 4 3 2 1

FC0415-03-X
ISBN: 2-0801-1251-1
Dépôt legal: 10/2003

Éditions Flammarion
26, rue Racine
75006 Paris
France

Printed in Italy by Canale